THE ULTIMATE GUIDE to *Dollywood*

Your Guide to THE BEST RIDES, RESTAURANTS, AND ATTRACTIONS AT *Dollywood*

ERIN K. BROWNE

Adams Media
New York • London • Toronto • Sydney • New Delhi

TO MY KIDS AND HUSBAND, MY FAVORITE ADVENTURE BUDDIES.

Adams Media
An Imprint of Simon & Schuster, LLC
100 Technology Center Drive
Stoughton, Massachusetts 02072

First Adams Media trade paperback edition September 2024

ADAMS MEDIA and colophon are registered trademarks of Simon & Schuster, LLC.

Simon & Schuster: Celebrating 100 Years of Publishing in 2024

For information about special discounts for bulk purchases, please contact Simon & Schuster Special Sales at 1-866-506-1949 or business@simonandschuster.com.

The Simon & Schuster Speakers Bureau can bring authors to your live event. For more information or to book an event, contact the Simon & Schuster Speakers Bureau at 1-866-248-3049 or visit our website at www.simonspeakers.com.

Interior design by Julia Jacintho
Interior images © 123RF
Interior maps and illustrations by Artisticco, LLC

Manufactured in the United States of America

10 9 8 7 6 5 4 3 2 1

Library of Congress Cataloging-in-Publication Data
Names: Browne, Erin K., author.
Title: The ultimate guide to Dollywood / Erin K. Browne.
Description: First Adams Media trade paperback edition. | Stoughton, Massachusetts: Adams Media, 2024. | Series: Unofficial Dollywood | Includes index.
Identifiers: LCCN 2024015753 | ISBN 9781507222225 (pb) | ISBN 9781507222232 (ebook)
Subjects: LCSH: Dollywood (Pigeon Forge, Tenn.)--Guidebooks. | Parton, Dolly.
Classification: LCC GV1853.3.T22 D653 2024 | DDC 791.06/8768893--dc23/eng/20240408
LC record available at https://lccn.loc.gov/2024015753

ISBN 978-1-5072-2222-5
ISBN 978-1-5072-2223-2 (ebook)

Contents

CHAPTER EIGHT

Wildwood Grove...175

CHAPTER NINE

Festivals...201

CHAPTER TEN

Other Dolly Properties...212

Introduction

Snuggled up to the Great Smoky Mountains in Pigeon Forge, Tennessee, Dollywood is more than a theme park; it's a special place where the thrill of roller coasters, the magic of live entertainment, and the warmth of good ol' Southern hospitality converge. Wander through the gates of the park and you'll find yourself making lasting memories and experiencing unforgettable adventures. Also, it's just a darn fun place to spend a day!

With rides that run the gamut from heart pounders that send adrenaline coursing through your veins to gentle journeys that immerse you in a theme, Dollywood has something for everyone. Beyond the rides, you can take in one of the dazzling shows that demonstrate the talents of performers who will leave you breathless with their artistry. Just like Dolly Parton's vibrant storytelling through her music, Dollywood is a place where heritage and tradition are celebrated. Be whisked away to the past in Craftsman's Valley, where skilled artisans create handcrafted goods right before your very eyes. Discover the rich culture of the Appalachian region through music, dance, and arts that pay homage to the area's history. Make sure you come hungry, because there are many opportunities for sampling mouthwatering Southern cuisine, from award-winning barbecue at Hickory House BBQ to the immensely popular cinnamon bread sold inside the historic Grist Mill.

But when you finally arrive on Showstreet and take a glimpse at a park map, you may feel a little overwhelmed. What to see? What to do? Where to begin?

In *The Ultimate Guide to Dollywood*, you'll be introduced to a hand-picked set of sights, sounds, tastes, and experiences to help guide you through the main park and other Dollywood properties. Whether you're a first-timer or frequent flier to the park, or you're an armchair traveler simply interested in learning more, this book is a super-helpful guide to the popular must-sees and the lesser-known hidden gems. Use it to plan your visit before you arrive, keep it tucked in your bag for easy reference during your stay, or share your favorite facts over some home cookin' with friends—whatever works best for you!

Organized as if you were actually walking through the park, each of the one hundred entries in this book includes a quick reference sidebar for important stats, a detailed overview, and other juicy tidbits to make sure you don't miss out on anything interesting. You'll also learn plenty of fun Dolly facts! Chapters 1 through 8 focus on specific areas within the main park, while Chapter 9 homes in on the roster of seasonal festivals in Dollywood. The final chapter explores a handful of attractions in Dollywood's Splash Country, details the fun and exhilarating experience of Dolly Parton's Stampede Dinner Attraction, and outlines the various resort accommodations available to visitors. By the time you're done reading, you'll be itching to pack your suitcase and head to East Tennessee.

Each chapter also includes a map of the areas discussed, so you can flip back to these handy references whether you're in the park or sitting at home taking a vicarious trip to the Smokies. Now grab a comfy chair and kick up your feet—it's time to take a deep dive into the best of what Dollywood has to offer!

CHAPTER ONE

Showstreet

★   ★

Showstreet is your grand introduction to Dollywood. It's the first place you'll step foot after passing through the front gates and the last place you'll see before saying goodbye at the end of your day. Visually, the area combines classic Southern charm with the glitz and glam of Hollywood, and Dolly's influence is apparent wherever you look. This cozy thoroughfare is the place to be to snack and shop your way through a variety of mountain-themed outlets and tasty eateries. You'll find giant ooey-gooey cinnamon rolls, country meals, and all of the Dolly merch you can handle. Showstreet is also known for its unique display of elaborate and ever-changing seasonal decor, and first-class live entertainment in two of the park's largest theaters.

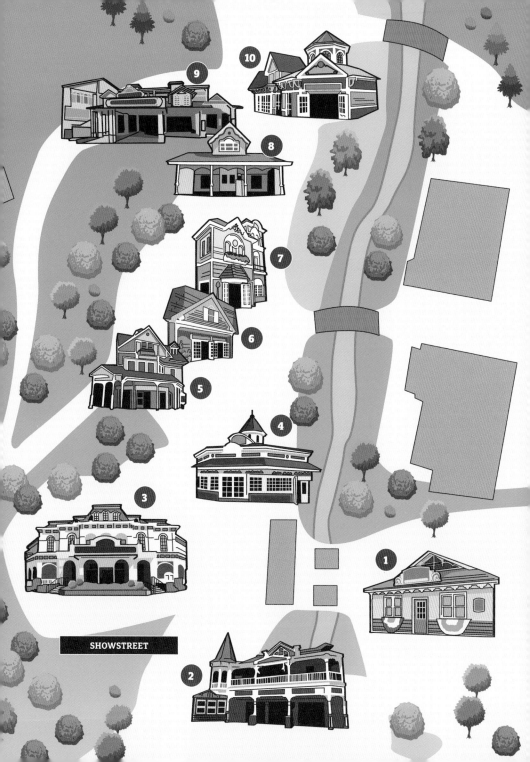

SHOWSTREET

1. Doggywood

WHAT: On-site kennels for non-service dogs while their owners enjoy Dollywood or Dollywood's Splash Country.

WHERE: Outside the park gates next to the Guest Services booths. Look for the Doggywood sign with the paw print "W"!

EXPERT TIP: Since space is limited, make reservations prior to your visit to guarantee availability.

▶ Why You Should See It

Dollywood has a lesser-known amenity for dog lovers visiting the park: its own kennel service! It's no surprise that Dolly would make sure doggies have a special place of their own given her lifelong love of canines. Dolly has been seen in public with her own beloved pups, hosted a pet-centric variety TV show called *Dolly Parton's Pet Gala* in February 2024, and has spoken affectionately about her relationship with her dogs in various interviews. She often reminisces about one special pet—Popeye, her Boston terrier—who was a particularly special companion in the early 1980s and who she credits with bringing happiness into some of her most difficult stages in life.

While the park welcomes registered service dogs in all areas, other pets are not allowed. Doggywood is located just outside Showstreet before you enter the front gates. Look for the cute little cottage with gingerbread trim. Available accommodations include twelve (4' × 6') kennel runs and four (5' × 5') cottages. Dogs that live in the same household can share a space for an additional small fee. Larger pups can enjoy the kennels, while the cottages are reserved for smaller dogs. The total weight of dogs in a single cottage cannot exceed 19 pounds.

The cottages are each uniquely decorated with wallpaper borders, artwork, and even a custom dog bed with headboard—just like a miniature hotel room! Up-to-date documentation for rabies and Bordetella vaccines are required to reserve a stay. Having kennel service right on the property is a huge convenience for guests who travel with dogs but aren't staying in town, or those who can't leave their pups in hotel rooms, rental cabins, or campers. Pups staying at Doggywood will have access to unlimited fresh water, but you'll need to provide food, toys, and other comfort items. While Dolly loves all kinds of pets, dogs are the only animals allowed to stay at the Doggywood facility, so please leave your feline and other furry friends at home!

▶ *Park Pointers*

While Doggywood hosts are happy to keep your pup comfy and safe while you have fun in the park, they cannot walk your dog for you. It's helpful to plan your day in Dollywood to include several trips past the front gate so that you can pop over to Doggywood and give your pooch a cuddle and a potty break. There is an enclosed walking area behind the kennels, and guests are asked to please clean up any waste after using the space.

Doggy Parton

Dolly's very first record—released in 1959—was "Puppy Love." Her love for pets has only grown stronger over the years, inspiring her to create her own line of pup apparel, accessories, and toys called Doggy Parton. The brand's ambassador is Dolly's beloved "god dog," a French bulldog named Billy the Kid (also featured in her book, *Dolly Parton's Billy the Kid Makes It Big*, released in April 2023). The line even includes a full-blown Dolly costume with a big blond wig and pink guitar!

2. Dollywood Emporium

= FAST FACTS =

WHAT: The largest shop in the park full of all things Dolly!

WHERE: Next to the main park entrance between Showstreet and the path to Timber Canyon. There's a second-story balcony with cream-colored railings behind the massive sign.

EXPERT TIP: Browse through the Emporium at the beginning of your day to get an idea of what's available and to help you spread out your spending as you explore the other shops in the park.

▶ Why You Should See It

If indulging in a little retail therapy sounds like the cherry on top of a perfect theme park day, then Dollywood Emporium has got you covered. Don't worry about accidentally missing out on this glorious shop, since you'll walk right through it to reach the main exit of the park. Remodeled for the 2022 season, the design features butterflies hanging from the ceiling, giant canvases of park attractions, and a lit-up marquee sign proclaiming what every guest already knows and feels: "I □ DW"! The shop's spacious layout allows guests to wander through different sections and admire a variety of items such as clothing, accessories, toys, collectibles, and other souvenirs to commemorate their time at Dollywood. The Emporium is a one-stop venue for Dollywood gifts and souvenirs.

From baseball caps and cowboy hats to T-shirts and other wearables, the designs change constantly, so it's not hard to find something you can't live without. Meander through the displays of printed coffee mugs, water bottles, and shot glasses, or take home a model train or miniature replica of your favorite ride. When you're riding the emotional high of a fun Dollywood day, it's hard to walk straight through the shop and out to the parking lots without making a purchase or two!

▶ Park Pointers

Dollywood has a "Package Pickup" service for purchases at other shops that total more than $25 and are made at least two hours before the park closes. If you buy something you don't want to carry around all day, let the shop host know and you will be given a card to redeem your items at the Package Pickup counter in Dollywood Emporium. If you're coming to Dollywood planning to go on a shopping spree, making use of this service won't limit your purchases to what you're able to lug through the park.

Get Measured

Not sure which rides your group can do together? The Centralized Measuring station next to Dollywood Emporium should be your first stop before hitting up any attractions. After being measured by a Dollywood host, guests are given a colored wristband that will help identify which rides they are tall enough to enjoy before getting in line.

3. Showstreet Palace Theater

FAST FACTS

WHAT: A comfortable indoor venue with a rotating schedule of shows.

WHERE: Straight ahead when you enter the main gate to the park. The brilliant marquee sign with the flashbulb border will light your way.

EXPERT TIP: Make a stop at the Dollywood sign in front of the theater for a professional photo before starting your day.

▶ Why You Should See It

When designing Showstreet, Dolly Parton envisioned an area that would encompass all the razzle-dazzle of Hollywood and showbiz. Dolly's personal expression through sparkly costumes, elaborate jewelry, and big blond wigs is echoed in the area's colorful theming. The shining beacon of Showstreet is the towering facade of the Showstreet Palace Theater. This 900-seat indoor auditorium opened during Dollywood's seventh season in 1992 and is home to some of the park's greatest entertainment acts. In front of the theater is the iconic Dollywood sign (with its signature butterfly-shaped "W") surrounded by a swath of gorgeous seasonal flowers. Inside, the padded bench seating and climate control make this a popular spot to take a break from either the summer heat or the winter chill. The Kingdom Heirs—a gospel singing group from the mountains of East Tennessee—is one of the recurring acts and has been performing in the theater for many years to rave reviews. The group's tenure on the property is so long-lived that they've been making audiences cheer since back when the park was named Silver Dollar City, before Dolly Parton ever came on board. In March 2023—during the brand-new I Will Always Love You Music Festival— the Songwriter's Showcase in the theater enabled up-and-coming songwriters and performers to reach a larger audience. In addition to live shows, you may even be able to catch the premiere of one of Dolly's newest films!

▶ Park Pointers

Download Dollywood's mobile app to see the show schedule the day of your visit and decide in advance which show(s) you'd like to see. The indoor theater is a nice reprieve from the weather, so plan to enjoy a show during the hottest (or coldest!) part of the day. Once you've settled on a showtime, use the app to set an alert so you don't forget while you're off elsewhere having fun. To cut the wait time and guarantee you'll have the best seats in the house, Showstreet Palace Theater participates in the TimeSaver program, allowing you to reserve priority seating to shows.

Record Breaker

Dolly's career as a songwriter and live performer is burnished with an impressive number of recognitions. Among them are her holding of ten Guinness World Records, the most recent of which include most studio albums released by a country singer, most entries on the US Top Country Albums chart by a female performer, and longest stint of number one hits by a female artist on the US Top Country Albums chart.

4. Spotlight Bakery

WHAT: Full-production bakery that serves fresh cookies, cupcakes, pastries, and other confections.

WHERE: On your right just after entering the park. The charming building wraps around the corner on Showstreet. Follow your nose and you can't miss the aroma wafting from the front doors.

EXPERT TIP: While Dolly has a sweet tooth for all kinds of desserts, she craves chocolate cake on her birthday. Indulge in a chocolate cupcake here on her (or your!) special day. Order it with a cold glass of milk to really do it Dolly-style!

▶ Why You Should See It

You won't get far past the front entrance of Dollywood before your senses are tickled with the tantalizing smells of cinnamon sugar and vanilla frosting. The source? Spotlight Bakery. Perched on the corner of Showstreet beneath a wood-siding cupola, Dollywood's own full-blown bakery is where the park's bakers and pastry chefs use their expertise and creativity to craft an impressive spread of delectable goodies. Choices include colossal cookies, cupcakes swirled high with frosting, apple turnovers, cheese Danish, fudgy brownies, jumbo muffins, and more. One standout guest favorite is the giant cinnamon rolls: heavenly swirls of yeast-leavened dough spread generously with flavored icing. More than three hundred cinnamon rolls are made from scratch and baked fresh every single morning to meet the high demand. As the seasons change, look for festive decorated sugar cookies, dipped Rice Krispies treats, and themed cupcake toppers. Dollywood bakers know their way around a piping bag and are always coming up with elaborate designs finished with sprinkles, sanding sugar, and other embellishments. Don't forget to sneak a peek at the giant apple pie on display, and if you have brought a few friends along with you, challenge yourselves to a group effort to finish a slice! Cool your heels at one of the small bistro tables inside, or take your dessert on the go as you enjoy the rest of what Showstreet has to offer.

▶ Park Pointers

If you are met with a long line at the Grist Mill when trying to score some of Dollywood's famous cinnamon bread, don't despair! Loaves of the award-winning treat can be purchased at Spotlight as well, served warm and ready to devour. There are also other varieties of freshly baked bread packaged up and ready to go, such as delectable apple butter bread or thick-sliced loaves of the butter crust bread used in the Meatloaf Stackers at Granny Ogle's Ham 'n' Beans. Because the bakery is located near the park entrance and exit, it's a perfect place to either grab a breakfast pastry as you start your day or cap off a visit with a tasty treat for the ride home.

The 25-Pound Apple Pie

To celebrate Dollywood's twenty-fifth season in 2010, Spotlight Bakery created a massive apple pie using a homemade filling of forty apples, a pound of butter, and a boatload of sugar and cinnamon baked until warm and ooey-gooey in a jumbo cast iron skillet. The pie was a smash hit, became a permanent menu item, and is available by the slice—each slice feeds four people—or by the whole pie...skillet included!

5. Showstreet Ice Cream

FAST FACTS

WHAT: Friendly ice cream shop serving hand-dipped scoops and yummy milkshakes.

WHERE: On the corner right across from Spotlight Bakery. The doorway of the pastel-colored building stands below signs promising what delights can be found inside.

EXPERT TIP: Seek out a table on the side porch of the shop for a quiet place to enjoy a treat away from the main street.

▶ Why You Should See It

Showstreet Ice Cream is Dollywood's nostalgic creamery and the best place in the park to get a frozen treat. Inside, Mayfield ice cream is hand scooped into cups, cones, or one of the shop's freshly made waffle bowls. Mayfield Dairy Farms is a well-loved regional dairy that started just down the road in Athens, Tennessee, in 1910. The brand produces high-quality milk, ice cream, and other dairy products throughout eastern Tennessee, northern Georgia, and northeastern Alabama. Some of the flavors available at Showstreet Ice Cream include vanilla, Smoky Mountain fudge, strawberry, mint chocolate chip, butter pecan, and strawberry cheesecake. For those with certain dietary needs, there are a limited number of no-sugar-added flavors offered as well. If you prefer sips to scoops, indulge in a thick and creamy milkshake—with whipped cream and a cherry, of course—

in vanilla, chocolate, or strawberry. For a more significant dessert, try a triple-scoop sundae with ice cream flavors of your choice topped with hot fudge or caramel, whipped cream, and a cherry, and served in a hand-crafted waffle bowl. If you have the kiddos in tow, have no fear: Sprinkles and other toppings can be added on request. There is limited seating inside, though if you walk to the other side of the building—through the Sweet Shoppe Candy Kitchen and The Southern Pantry—you'll find an area next to the windows with places to sit. Outdoor tables and rocking chairs are available as well.

▶ *Park Pointers*

Showstreet Ice Cream creates delicious ice cream combinations using crispy Liège waffles. Similar to their Belgian cousin, Liège waffles differ in that they have irregular shapes and use a thicker, bread dough–like batter dotted with crystallized bits of pearl sugar. When the finished product comes out of the waffle iron, it has a crunchy exterior and a soft, chewy center. You get to pick the ice cream flavors to create any combo of tastes that you want! Some options you may see include chocolate-dipped Liège waffles sprinkled with chopped pistachio nuts and sandwiched with ice cream, and a single waffle piled high with scoops of ice cream, cookie or peanut butter cup pieces, chocolate drizzle, and whipped cream. Dealing with a bit of brain freeze? Complement your frozen treat with a hot beverage such as rich hot chocolate, coffee, or cappuccino.

 ### Made for Dolly

The Ohio-based and wildly popular ice cream brand Jeni's Splendid Ice Creams created a special 2021 flavor in collaboration with Dolly based on her favorite Jeni's flavor, Strawberry Buttermilk. The exclusive flavor, Strawberry Pretzel Pie, crashed the company's website and sold out within minutes during its initial release.

6. Sweet Shoppe Candy Kitchen

FAST FACTS

WHAT: Dedicated candy shop as sweet as its name, featuring both fresh-made and prepackaged candies.

WHERE: Right in between The Southern Pantry and Show-street Ice Cream. So many goodies all in a row!

EXPERT TIP: The chocolate-covered frozen cheesecake is a must-try. Imagine a thick slice of rich cheesecake, graham cracker crust and all, super chilled and completely enrobed in a layer of chocolate.

▶ Why You Should See It

Dollywood's colorful candy kitchen is a whimsical wonderland of sugary delights. Skilled artisans work their magic in the bustling shop creating a variety of treats. Take a peek inside the display case to see the offerings of the day—they change all the time. Some items you might come across include peanut butter buckeye balls, truffles, chocolate peanut clusters, old-fashioned potato candy, cookies-and-cream candy bark, and chocolate-dipped confections. Don't forget about the thick bars of home-made fudge—the park serves up to 2,000 pieces every day—available in both classic and creative flavors such as salted caramel, orange cream, and raspberry lemonade. Alongside the fragrant fudge, rows of caramel apples are a sight to behold as they are dipped, drizzled, and made even more colorful with sprinkles. This candied fruit is a park favorite, with up to 950 apples sold each day!

Past the display case you will encounter a vast array of homemade taffy in a seemingly endless number of flavors. The basics such as strawberry, peppermint, and chocolate are covered, but you'll also find some surprising varieties like maple bacon, root beer float, and buttered popcorn! On the opposite wall is a cornucopia of packaged candies, including Tennessee-made Goo Goo Clusters and MoonPies, as well as vintage favorites.

▶ *Park Pointers*

Hang a right when you enter the candy shop from the outside and walk through the building it shares with The Southern Pantry. Prior to the 2024 season, you could see the taffy pulling and packaging machines in a demonstration area located behind the painted swirled railings (the machines have since been moved). Dollywood's expert candymakers can create over 1,200 pieces of taffy from a single batch—that's a lotta candy!

If you happen to see master craftsman Linda Rice behind the counter, make sure to say hello. Linda has been making candy at the park since it was named Silver Dollar City and she has perfected every recipe used in the shop. The covered porch outside the candy shop is a hidden gem, perfect for enjoying a treat and people-watching. Relax on a wooden rocking chair beneath lazily turning ceiling fans and enjoy the fresh flowers in the plant boxes lining the wooden railings. The porch provides welcome shady relief during hot summer days in East Tennessee.

 ### Three in One

The Southern Pantry, Sweet Shoppe Candy Kitchen, and Showstreet Ice Cream are all connected from the inside, so you can browse all three shops at once without stepping foot outside.

7. The Southern Pantry

═══ FAST FACTS ═══

WHAT: Specialty kitchen shop that sells canned preserves, sauces, baking mixes, and decor.

WHERE: Directly across from the Showstreet gazebo. Look for the giant fork and spoon flanking the front doors!

EXPERT TIP: This is a perfect place to pick up gifts for your foodie friends back home. Everything is shelf-stable and travels well!

▶ Why You Should See It

If you love to be creative in the kitchen, The Southern Pantry is a great way to take home a little taste of the Smokies. All the items sold here are inspired by Southern traditions to capture the flavors and overall essence of the region. Inside the cozy shop, you'll find rows upon rows of colorful jars and bottles stacked on white-painted wood hutches lining the walls. Start reading the labels and you'll discover a variety of fresh fruit preserves from classic options like strawberry, raspberry, and blackberry to more unique combinations such as blueberry moonshine and peach amaretto pecan. Dolly herself is a huge fan of preserved fruits, and she even has a killer prize-winning recipe for canned pickled peaches from her aunt Lily Owens (look it up sometime!). Also available is a collection of jarred vegetables and specialty sauces and dips such as tangy barbecue glazes and exotic salsas. If you're a caffeine lover, take home a bag of fresh-ground

Dollywood coffee in fun flavors like Southern Pecan and Caramel Mudslide. To complement the delectable food offerings, the shop also features a curated selection of kitchen decor. You can find items such as decorative hand towels, country aprons, mugs, and artisanal utensils to add a touch of charm and elegance to your kitchen.

▶ Park Pointers

Hidden throughout Dollywood are signs that commemorate employees—called "hosts"—who have been working in the park for thirty years or more. The tradition began during 2016—Dollywood's thirtieth season—and continues to this day. The Showstreet area surrounding The Southern Pantry is a great place to start keeping an eye out for these signs, because it's easy to miss them! The hidden tributes are disguised as wanted posters, framed art, or old-fashioned advertisements. The hosts' names and year they began their employment are hidden somewhere in the signs, and you'll have to do some sleuthing to figure those out. For example, hidden next door to The Southern Pantry you'll find a placard for a piano factory owned by a man named David Brooks. While Mr. Brooks doesn't actually own a company, he *is* a piano player and has performed and served as a musical director for several shows in Dollywood for more than three decades. He began working in 1988, which is disguised in the statement "Standard 88 Keys on All Models" on the advertisement. While making your way through the park, see how many of these signs you can find!

8. Front Porch Café

WHAT: Cozy full-service restaurant serving up steaming plates of Southern favorites.

WHERE: On the corner of Market Square. Look for the colorful mailboxes in front of the farmhouse-style building.

EXPERT TIP: The crispy fried green tomatoes are a guest favorite that shouldn't be missed. They're served with sweet-roasted red pepper sauce and basil oil and topped with crumbled goat cheese.

▶ Why You Should See It

Sitting down to a meal at Front Porch Café is like going over to your mamaw's house for Sunday supper. The country-style house is warm and inviting with wood-plank tables, farmhouse chairs, and walls adorned with murals and framed artwork. Dolly's vision for the restaurant encompasses her love for front porch sittin' and sweet tea sippin' with her family and friends, where she believes some of the biggest dreams are made. As one of the park's few table service venues, the Café has friendly waitstaff who wear gingham tops and exude Southern charm. Though the menu is notorious for undergoing changes, some items you might see are smothered country-fried steak, herb-roasted chicken, and a variety of fresh garden salads, crispy chicken sandwiches, pork belly BLTs, and grilled hamburgers.

Bread options in the past have included buttery garlic Cheddar biscuits, homestyle buttermilk biscuits, and Southern corn bread. Freshly brewed iced tea is always available—try the sweet peach flavor for something different! Unlike many of the other restaurants in Dollywood, Front Porch Café has the convenience of its own public restroom facilities right inside the building (they're small, so expect a line during busier times).

▶ Park Pointers

If you're a longtime visitor to Dollywood, you may know this restaurant by its former name, Backstage Restaurant. In 2017, the venue underwent a major renovation, name change, and reimagined menu. The establishment as it exists today is responsive to guest feedback and frequently makes updates and adds new dishes, making the Café worthy of repeat visits for a chance to try something new. The place can get very busy during peak times of the day, so plan to eat in between typical mealtimes to avoid the bulk of the crowds. You can also stop at the host station after the park opens to add your name to a reservation list. Front Porch Café can make accommodations for almost any food allergy or dietary need. Chat with your server once seated to receive personalized information from the chef regarding your individual requirements. As the closest indoor restaurant to the park gates, you can either begin your day here with an early lunch or take a rest after you've had your fill of rides and entertainment with dinner after dark.

A La Mode

In Dolly's cookbook, *Dolly's Dixie Fixin's*, she shares a recipe for peach cobbler that her stylist and personal assistant, Ira Parker, used to make for the crew during a 2005 tour. Dolly says that it tastes best when served with vanilla ice cream and whipped cream. Try it!

9. DP's Celebrity Theater

═══ FAST FACTS ═══

WHAT: Dollywood's largest theater, because you need a big theater for big shows!

WHERE: Up the steep hill on Showstreet, behind Front Porch Café.

EXPERT TIP: This theater doesn't do small or simple, so if a show is on the schedule here, it's a good one. See them all!

▶ Why You Should See It

DP's Celebrity Theater ("DP" for "Dolly Parton"!), the park's largest indoor venue, seats 1,739 people. Opening in 1988, the theater debuted with "Showcase of Stars," a celebrity concert series that packed full houses to see the big names who traveled to Pigeon Forge to perform. The popular series returned for Dollywood's thirtieth anniversary and included performances by Dolly herself. The concerts required a separate ticket purchase, with sales benefiting Dolly Parton's Imagination Library. Usually, the live shows at Dollywood are included with your park ticket, but this series was an exception. Since then, the theater continues to host celebrity concert weekends, most of them only available to Gold and Diamond season passholders. Names like Natalie Grant, Jo Dee Messina, Ricky Skaggs, and the Gatlin Brothers have been on the schedule in recent years. During the holidays, *Christmas in the Smokies* is said by some to be the absolute best festive show in the park and will leave you full of warm and fuzzies. You can always count on the Celebrity Theater to have something awesome going on inside! If you have a TimeSaver pass, don't be afraid to use it to reserve priority seating to your favorite shows.

▶ Park Pointers

Whatever you do, go straight to the *Gazillion Bubble Show* at DP's Celebrity Theater during Dollywood's Smoky Mountain Summer Celebration. Combining art, science, and entertainment, the show features dazzling displays of bubble artistry. Watch as intricate bubble sculptures, bubbles within bubbles, and massive bubbles that completely engulf audience members are created live. Advanced lighting effects and laser technology enhance the visual spectacle. The show includes interactive elements where children and adults can climb onstage and participate in the bubble magic, and just about everyone in the audience will be able to grab and pop bubbles as they rain down from the ceiling. Since 2007, Fan Yang's family of award-winning (and Guinness World Records–holding!) bubble artists have been traveling the world, delighting people by the thousands— both live and on TV programs. Dollywood visitors are *huge* fans of this show, bringing it back year after year. Go see it!

10. Traditions

────── FAST FACTS ──────

WHAT: Retail shop specializing in products and apparel inspired by Southern traditions.

WHERE: In the Market Square area of Showstreet, just past the bridge that leads across the creek to Jukebox Junction. The scripted sign is adorned with a compass above the French doors that beckon you to come in and browse.

EXPERT TIP: Long wait at Front Porch Café? Traditions is just a few steps down the path and is perfect to help you pass the time while waiting for your table.

▶ Why You Should See It

Traditions is a charming indoor shop that offers a delightful array of Southern-inspired items. From colorful T-shirts printed with funny quotes to trendy outfits and adorable accessories adorned with whimsical designs, this boutique is a haven for those seeking to express the spirit of the South through fashion. When you walk through the front doors, look up to appreciate the windowed turret roof that adds to the nostalgic vibe. Two brands that are featured prominently inside Traditions are Simply Southern and Kerusso. Simply Southern is a company founded in Greensboro, North Carolina. The brand is known for its bright and cheery colors, graphic T-shirts, and cutesy extras. Kerusso is a faith-based company that started in 1987 and focuses on products featuring Christian messaging and symbols. Traditions carries Dollywood-exclusive products from these two brands and more, including vibrant fashion pieces and catchy Dolly-themed apparel. This shop is also great for picking up canvas belt bags—ideal for a hands-free day in the park—as well as water bottles, coffee mugs, key chains, and more. Both adult and youth clothing sizes are available, so you can pick something up for the youngest Dolly fans in your life as well.

▶ *Park Pointers*

Dolly wanted her beloved park to have connections to her personal life, her childhood, her memories, and her music as much as possible, and that desire is present from such details as the theme of a gift shop to the more obvious associations present throughout Dollywood. Once you're done browsing at Traditions, check out Gazebo Gifts, a small outdoor stand mere feet away to find the latest and greatest exclusive Dollywood merchandise. If it's new, seasonal, limited, or any other adjective to signify "brand spankin' new," it'll be there. While shopping, keep in mind that Dollywood season passholders (Gold level or higher) can take advantage of a percentage discount on select purchases inside the park. Specific details of discounts and eligibility may change, so check the Dollywood app or website for the most up-to-date details on passholder benefits.

Dolly's Traditions

Dolly is no stranger to traditions, especially around the holidays. Every year, she gets a live Christmas tree because her daddy always took her and her siblings to chop down a tree. Her mama decorated the tree with whatever she could find, like buttons and feathers. Because they had no electricity for lights, they made popcorn garlands, and she keeps that tradition going still today.

CHAPTER TWO

★ Rivertown Junction ★

Rivertown Junction is a rustic haven with a serene ambience nestled among a peaceful pond and the babbling waters of Middle Creek. Here you can indulge in some of Dollywood's tastiest on-the-go snacks, sit down to a home-cooked family-style Southern meal, or bite into a giant corn dog while tapping your feet to some authentic bluegrass in a casual outdoor theater. Rivertown Junction lives up to its name with its main attraction: a white water rafting adventure that the whole family can enjoy! Whether you're walking through a springtime floral wonderland, enjoying the vibrant autumn colors, warming up the winter with thousands of holiday lights, or chillin' in the shade during a hot Tennessee summer, Rivertown Junction is an awesome place to experience all of Dollywood's vibes.

RIVERTOWN JUNCTION

1. Market Square
BIG SKILLET

FAST FACTS

WHAT: Open-air food stand crafting creative dishes cooked on what are sure to be the biggest skillets you have ever seen.

WHERE: On the main path between Showstreet and Rivertown Junction. Let your nose be your guide.

EXPERT TIP: Arrive soon after the park opens to avoid longer lines. They form quickly!

▶ Why You Should See It

Market Square BIG SKILLET is a place that demands to be seen (and smelled) from its prominent location right in the middle of the path as you leave Showstreet. You'd have to make a special effort to avoid the wide, covered walkway that borders Rivertown Junction. This is where the sizzle meets the griddle; the aromas of sausage, peppers, and onions emanate from the massive skillets as Dollywood hosts whip up the stand's signature sandwiches and bowls. Among the most popular dishes are perfectly seasoned cheesesteak sandwiches and piping-hot sausage and potato "skillets." Kitchens are positioned on either side of the walkway, ensuring a clear view of the trademarked skillets used to fry and sauté ingredients to perfection. Large stainless offset spatulas are positioned around each skillet for flipping and turning the substantial mounds of ingredients. Even if you're not hungry, it's still fun to stop and snap a photo of the most gigantic skillet you'll ever see in your life!

The Market Square area is peppered with picnic tables mounted with umbrellas on both sides of the walkway, making it fairly easy to find a place to sit to enjoy your food or just take a rest before venturing on. The paved open-air spot is conveniently located close to other food stands selling Dollywood's iconic funnel cakes and kettle corn, so you might want to save a little room for some additional treats once you've finished your skillet creation.

▶ *Park Pointers*

Menu boards flanking the walkway as you approach it from either direction show mouthwatering photos of the limited dishes currently available. The menu boards above the cashier station display the classics that are available all the time. Another focus of BIG SKILLET is newer innovations, and a recent offering that's been getting all kinds of attention is the potato tornado. What the heck is a potato tornado? It's what happens when you take a plain potato and spiral cut it around a skewer. But the fun doesn't stop there: The whole thing then gets deep-fried, seasoned, and topped with anything under the sun. Available toppings vary, and you might see tornadoes with cheese and bacon, salted maple flavoring, or even one that's wrapped around a hot dog instead of a skewer! This is a place that you gotta try at least once during a Dollywood day.

Spuds 'n' Studs

Dolly, being the unapologetic firecracker that she is, has stated that her two weaknesses in life are food and men. In that order. Dolly has admitted that potatoes tend to ruin her diets, and she loves them any way you can make 'em: baked, fried, mashed, or even rolled up with peanut butter and sliced into potato candy pinwheels.

2. Crossroads Funnel Cakes

FAST FACTS

WHAT: Funnel cakes, funnel cakes, funnel cakes!

WHERE: Tucked away in the corner adjacent to Market Square BIG SKILLET. The open-air stand has a green, white, and red awning that shades the order window.

EXPERT TIP: Funnel cakes are fun to eat, but they're also messy! Claim a table under a red umbrella in the nearby picnic area to chow down more tidily.

▶ Why You Should See It

Whether you're at a carnival, county fair, or theme park, funnel cakes top the list of must-have indulgent treats! Dollywood's crispy-fried swirls of sweet batter are some of the best around, so stopping by Crossroads should always be part of your park itinerary. When you enter Rivertown Junction, that sweet, irresistible aroma of freshly fried dough hits you like a warm summer breeze. It's a siren call that you can't resist, so any effort to do so is futile.

The funnel cakes here are lattices of crispy goodness that are served either plain, with a sprinkle of powdered sugar, or topped with your choice of strawberries, Oreo cookie crumbles, chocolate sauce, or whipped topping. Funnel cakes are like a blank canvas for flavor creativity and are a perfect vehicle for all kinds of toppings. The menu occasionally adds limited-edition flavors as well, so you'll always want to cruise through and see what they're cooking up on any given day. Red velvet—using a special bright red batter with that familiar buttermilk tang and light note of chocolate—was a huge hit in the past, and made for a stunning presentation with its bright color and contrasting snow-white powdered sugar and cream cheese drizzle. Then there was the Fruity Pebbles version that was a whole carnival in every bite, with its confetti-like presentation featuring the brightly colored cereal, a mountain of whipped cream, and rainbow sprinkles. These unique funnel cakes are some of the prettiest treats that Dollywood serves, so you might want to snap a photo before digging in to be able to show everyone back home. You might get a request to bring one back with you, and while you are welcome to try, funnel cakes are always best when eaten still warm and crisp straight out of the fryer.

▶ *Park Pointers*

During the regular season, Dollywood produces a staggering 87,000 funnel cakes. If you stacked all of those on top of each other, they would reach a height of approximately 7,250 feet. That's taller than the highest point in the Smoky Mountains, Clingmans Dome, which stands at 6,643 feet! The 2023 season saw two brand-new products added to the Crossroads menu. The first, Mountain Fry Bread, is made from a basic dough rolled out and fried up until golden, crispy, and bubbly, then topped with cinnamon sugar and finished with a drizzle of honey, a squeeze of lemon, and a sprinkling of powdered sugar. The other, Spiced Apple Stack, is a tower of funnel cakes layered with cinnamon sugar and apple pie filling and topped with caramel sauce and whipped topping.

 ### Splinter's Funnel Cakes

Hit by a funnel cake craving while on the opposite end of the park? Go to Splinter's in Wilderness Pass for a similar menu—festival flavors included!

3. Country Cookers—
Kettle Korn

FAST FACTS

WHAT: Walk-up snack stand selling Dollywood's famous salty-sweet Kettle Korn in flavors spanning from basic to bold!

WHERE: Past the Market Square walkway in Rivertown Junction, across from the northern end of the large pond.

EXPERT TIP: Before making your showtime for one of the many live performances on the property, pick up a bag of Kettle Korn for munchin' on something more special than plain buttered popcorn while you watch.

▶ Why You Should See It

It might be either the *poppity-pop-pop* sound or the smell of fresh popcorn coming from the huge kettles inside the Country Cookers stand that lures you over for a closer look. The contrast between salty and sweet adds complexity and depth to the flavor while keeping your taste receptors fully engaged with each bite. Dollywood's popcorn masters look like they're performing science experiments in their elbow-length rubber gloves, face shields, and thick aprons as they wield large wooden paddles and stir vats of fresh Kettle Korn. Yup, it's spelled with a "k" in the Dollywood world! The process of creating Dollywood's signature snack is simple but precise.

First, the kettles are heated until very hot. Oil and corn kernels are added and allowed to get to the point where the first few kernels are just starting to pop. Then it's time to sweeten the pot, literally, with some granulated sugar. The sugar makes contact with the high-heat environment of the kettle and caramelizes, resulting in the delightful sweet crunch of the finished product. The popcorn is stirred constantly until every piece is perfectly popped, then finished with some salt and quickly transferred out of the kettle and into the hands of snack-loving Dollywood guests. Are you one such guest? You will be after your first taste of this expertly made crunchy snack.

▶ Park Pointers

Country Cookers is all about keeping things fresh, in more ways than one! Not only are you guaranteed a perfectly crunchy batch of Kettle Korn that's cooked on-site all day, every day, but you can choose from an ever-changing variety of flavors and colors depending on the time of year you visit. You might see red and green Kettle Korn during Dollywood's Smoky Mountain Christmas festival along with winter flavors like hot cocoa and peppermint, or autumnal colors with fall flavors like salted caramel and pumpkin spice during the Harvest Festival. Grab a bag early in your day for easy, not-too-heavy snacking that's portable, tasty, and oh so satisfying. This is a treat that travels well, so go ahead and purchase an extra bag or two and take a taste of Dollywood back home with you.

All in the Family

Dolly believes in making employees feel respected and heard when new ideas are brought to the table, and that includes flavors of Kettle Korn! To celebrate the 2023 opening of the new roller coaster, Big Bear Mountain, a blueberry, strawberry, and banana mix was created called Mountain Berry Crunch. The flavor was an idea dreamed up by an operations manager at the park.

4. Mountain Blown Glass

═══ FAST FACTS ═══

WHAT: Unique shop selling beautiful handcrafted glass pieces blown into shape right before your eyes.

WHERE: Just before the train tracks cross the path from Rivertown Junction to Owens Farm.

EXPERT TIP: Create your own custom glass ornament to have shipped home or picked up at the end of the day.

▶ Why You Should See It

A visit to Mountain Blown Glass starts by walking up to a covered viewing area outdoors where you can see Dollywood's artisans shape molten glass into beautiful items. Watch as liquid glass is collected onto a blowpipe from a furnace that maintains heat at a staggering 2,000°F. The lump of glowing material is rolled, blown, and molded, and then returned to the furnace—also called a crucible—many times to keep the glass malleable. To add some extra pizzazz, the hot glass can be rolled into tiny bits of colored glass called "frit" that are melted into the base before a final shaping into what will be the finished product. The piece is cooled slowly in an annealing oven over a period of hours, given a final polish, and then it's good to go. Inside the shop, you can purchase many of the creations made right in the park using this same process, like figurines, vases, pitchers, ornaments, oil dispensers, and so much more.

The coolest part of Mountain Blown Glass is that you can customize your very own Christmas ornament and you even get to help make it! With the help of an expert glassblower, you'll decide exactly what you want your ornament to look like, including choosing the base color of the glass and which colors of frit, if any, you want to add. While the artist rolls the blowpipe, you're given a tube with a disposable mouthpiece that connects to the end of the pipe. You'll be instructed to blow even breaths into the tube to make your ornament come to life! It's a special experience to watch the molten glass expand and take shape—with your breathing as the driving force—into something beautiful.

▶ Park Pointers

The craftspeople who demonstrate their talents at Dollywood aren't just actors, they're the real deal, so you know you're getting a true behind-the-scenes look at how these lovely pieces are created. Visiting this shop isn't only about retail therapy, it's also educational. The artisans are always happy to answer questions and share their passion for this ancient art form, making it a memorable stop during your Dollywood visit. When browsing inside, you'll want to keep a close watch on the exploring fingers of little ones since just about everything is breakable. It is an entire shop full of nothing but glass, after all! Mountain Blown Glass updates its inventory seasonally, so there's always something new to see. For example, during the fall months, you'll see all colors of glittery pumpkins with curly stems. During Christmas, expect Santas, snowmen, and the like. There's a high-end feel to these exquisite one-of-a-kind items, so if you need a gift or souvenir that's a little fancier than the basic fare, remember this place!

Dolly's Glass Unicorn

In her home, Dolly has a special blown glass unicorn that was created just for her by the master glassblowers in Dollywood. She finds the whole process fascinating and interesting to watch.

5. Aunt Granny's Restaurant

FAST FACTS

WHAT: The best sit-down restaurant in the park for a delicious traditional Southern comfort meal, served family-style and all you can eat!

WHERE: Across from the big pond (look for fountains and a waterwheel) in Rivertown Junction.

EXPERT TIP: Don't miss the hand-breaded Southern fried chicken and corn pudding.

▶ Why You Should See It

For the truest Southern supper experience in Dollywood, get over to Aunt Granny's! From the painted rafter ceiling and honey oak country tables to the hanging cast iron cookware and copper pots, you know you're in for some authentic down-home cookin' before you even get a chance to take a seat and put your napkin in your lap. From the current day's menu, guests choose three entrées and four side dishes for the table to share. At the end of the meal, each person gets to choose a dessert. Drink orders go in first, and then some fresh bread is brought to the table. You might get warm garlic Cheddar biscuits, homemade Southern-style biscuits, or corn bread. All are divine. Favorite entrées include crispy fried chicken, seasoned fried catfish, and tender beef pot roast. Some of the standout side dishes include corn pudding, Southern green beans, mashed potatoes, and creamy mac and cheese. Everything is served fresh and hot from the kitchen and sure to leave everyone going "mmm-mmm, good!" after sampling it.

Save some room for dessert, because the options—like banana pudding, dirt cake parfait, and seasonal fruit crumble—are tempting. Unlimited bread service and fountain beverages are included in the price of the meal. On your way into or out of the building, check out the water flume near the small pond—look for the barrel full of holes the flume empties into. The flume carries water through an elevated stream constructed throughout the park, powering both the Grist Mill up in Craftsman's Valley and the unique Harvey Water Clock structure not far from the restaurant.

▶ Park Pointers

Aunt Granny's used to be an all-you-can-eat buffet. Guests were seated at their table and then given free access to visit the buffet as often as they liked. Following the onset of the COVID-19 pandemic, the restaurant shifted to family-style dining to accommodate changing safety recommendations. Free refills are available for all dishes ordered, however, so you'll still be able to fill your belly as much as you want! As soon as you reach the bottom of a serving bowl, your friendly server will be by to ask if you'd like another. It's up to you to decide if you have room left for more or not, but sometimes the food at Aunt Granny's is just so darn good it's hard to not accept another helpin'. Because this is one of Dollywood's most popular restaurants, the wait times can be lengthy on high-attendance days or at peak mealtimes. Visit the host stand early in the day to see about getting your name on a reservation list and cut down on your wait time.

A Name with Meaning

Dolly Parton was born the fourth child of twelve, and she helped care for her younger brothers and sisters. Once grown, Dolly never had any children of her own and became quite close with all of her nieces and nephews, who gave her the loving nickname "Aunt Granny."

6. Mountain Laurel HOME

FAST FACTS

WHAT: Country-chic home accessories, handmade soaps, and decor in a beautiful retail setting.

WHERE: The most prominent shop in Rivertown Junction, with a working waterwheel marking its location.

EXPERT TIP: Needing some help with your decorating skills? Study the professional tablescapes and room vignettes in the store—or take photos—for ideas about how to set up your own home.

▶ Why You Should See It

Mountain Laurel HOME is one store you need to visit at Dollywood even if you don't plan on buying anything—it's just that picturesque! When you walk inside, it's hard to miss the shop's most eye-catching feature: a large indoor-outdoor waterwheel. As the wheel turns and the paddles dip into the flowing water, you'll hear a gentle and rhythmic splashing. The water's constant motion produces a melodious babbling reminiscent of a mountain creek. The inventory at the store combines sophisticated elegance with Southern charm. Enjoy the fresh fragrance of handmade soaps and artisanal candles, run your hands over delicate table linens and soft blankets, or ogle at gold-trimmed serving dishes and stemware. Through the stacked stone and beam flat archway are even more wonders to behold. If the weather is inclement during your visit, Mountain Laurel is a great place to duck inside and wait out the elements. You'll forget that it's yucky outside after a few minutes of perusing. The fence bordering the creek outside is a great spot to stop for a rest and view the waterwheel and fountains. Hang out long enough and you may meet some of the duck families that make Dollywood their home.

▶ Park Pointers

The items in Mountain Laurel HOME frequently change to reflect the current season. During the fall, you might see rustic pumpkins and squash, faux chrysanthemums, or not-so-spooky skeletons and ghosts for Halloween. Christmas is when the store really comes alive with everything you need to host an impressive holiday party. Browse opulent place settings and ornate centerpieces or pick out the perfect ornament from the exquisitely decorated Christmas trees filling the shop with warm twinkling lights. The shop's name comes from a blooming shrub that is found all over the Smoky Mountains. Mountain laurel has fragile pink and white flowers that can be seen in full bloom in May and June. It is often confused with another bloom common in the Smokies—rhododendron—that blooms slightly later. The laurels in the mountains are known for breaking records with their size, some reaching towering tree-like proportions, full of clusters of blossoms.

7. Butterfly Strings Music Store

FAST FACTS

WHAT: Rivertown Junction's 2023 addition featuring music-themed merchandise from Dolly and other classic performers.

WHERE: Gable-roofed building with painted-blue wood siding behind Aunt Granny's Restaurant and Dolly's Tennessee Mountain Home.

EXPERT TIP: Fans of top artists from the Sun Records label like Johnny Cash and Elvis Presley will find all kinds of fun things to explore!

▶ Why You Should See It

Opened in time for the 2023 season, Butterfly Strings Music Store pays tribute to some of America's most well-known musical artists, most of whom Dolly Parton has inspired or was inspired by. Once through the glass-paned French doors that mark the entrance, direct your gaze upward to the memorabilia circling the store. You can find vinyl albums, vintage guitar cases, instruments, and concert posters from some of country music's most celebrated performers, past and present. As for the items up for purchase, you can find goods for the home, like triple-woven throw blankets, printed coffee mugs, and accent pillows. Also available are branded apparel and accessories including jewelry, cowboy and baseball hats, and a plethora of quirky T-shirts. More classic souvenirs like hand-carved magnets, key chains, stickers, and ornaments also adorn the shelves. If you want to dress for the stage (or maybe just for attending a concert) you can pick up some specialized performance costumes fit for Dolly herself, like bejeweled trousers, sparkled fringe tank tops, and sequin-covered skirts and jackets. The shop's most unique offering, though, is a colorful assortment of authentic ukuleles just like the one that Miss Lillian, "The Chicken Lady," strums to elicit smiles from passersby in Craftsman's Valley.

▶ Park Pointers

Butterfly Strings was installed in the building that previously housed Rivertown Christmas Cottage. If you've visited Dollywood in the past, you may feel bummed at first about Rivertown Christmas Cottage being no more, but don't worry! Dolly knows her visitors love to get their holiday cheer year-round and has come up with a solution. Smoky Mountain Christmas Shop, Dollywood's newest spot for all things tinsel, now shares a location with Valley Wood Carvers in Craftsman's Valley. So head on up the hill a ways to have yourself a holly jolly (or holly Dolly?) Christmas any time of the year.

The Chicken Lady

Miss Lillian, better known as "The Chicken Lady," is the fictional owner of Miss Lillian's Mill House in Craftsman's Valley. She meanders around making up songs on the fly, spreading happiness to and taking photos with guests who wander by. Her typical uniform consists of a country-style dress printed with chickens and topped with a vibrant apron. Her colorful shoes with mismatched laces and her endless collection of quirky eyeglasses are also signature accessories. A "be-chickened" hat and a pair of lace fingerless gloves—she has to be able play her ukulele or banjo, after all—complete the ensemble.

8. Harvey Water Clock

WHAT: A large clock that keeps time while being powered only by flowing water.

WHERE: At the intersection of Rivertown Junction and the base of Craftsman's Valley, near where the Dollywood Express railroad tracks cross the path.

EXPERT TIP: Take a picture with the clock during each visit to the park as a time stamp to remember your trips.

▶ Why You Should See It

The unique Harvey Water Clock is not an official attraction listed on any Dollywood map, making it a fun hidden gem that's worthy of a look. What makes the clock so special is that it is not powered by electricity, batteries, or solar energy. Instead, the hands of each of the four faces are moved only by the water that flows over and through the mechanisms of the clock, marking the year, month, day, and time. To get the full effect of this amazing timepiece, start at the top of Craftsman's Valley and notice the water trough raised above the creek running along the middle of the path. The trough draws water up from the creek and carries it all the way down the hill to power both the water clock and the nearby historic Grist Mill. Observe how the water flows though the clock, activating each clockface in different, specific periods of time using a clock part known as a centrifugal, or "fly-ball," governor. While an attractive fixture all year round, the pond surrounding the clock makes for a beautiful scene in springtime (and especially for picture takin') when highlighted by flowers, topiaries, and other seasonal decor.

▶ Park Pointers

The Harvey Water Clock was patented way back in 1798. The clockface that indicates the current year only shows a single decade: the 1880s. While this may seem peculiar, there's a reason behind it. Dollywood was known as Silver Dollar City when the 1880s-themed property was purchased by the Herschend brothers in 1976. The park's name was changed to Dollywood in 1986, though there is currently another Silver Dollar City, owned by the Herschend brothers and located in Branson, Missouri. The Missouri park also features a Harvey Water Clock that only shows the decade between 1880 and 1890. This is a tribute to both the nineteenth-century theme of the Herschend brothers' current Silver Dollar City and the previous version of Dollywood. To correctly tell the year, look at only the last digit of the year on the clock. For example, the year 2024 is indicated as 1884. When the clock hand gets all the way around the face, the decade starts over again, so in the year 2030, the clock will read 1880!

 Details Matter

One of the original designers of the park, Andy Miller, was known for his attention to little details and commitment to historical accuracy. He is credited with many of the architectural designs and theming of Dollywood, and the idea for including the water clock in the modern-day park is one of them. Long-time employees of Dollywood like to call his contributions "Andyisms."

9. Dolly's Tennessee Mountain Home

======== FAST FACTS ========

WHAT: A replica of Dolly Parton's humble mountain home where she grew up in the mountains of East Tennessee.

WHERE: Perched among lush landscaping and flowers in Rivertown Junction. There's a long ramp on one side leading to the two entrances to the building.

EXPERT TIP: Squint hard and see if you can read the labels on the tins of vintage kitchen products on the "pantry" shelves.

▶ Why You Should See It

Walking through the re-creation of Dolly's childhood home on Locust Ridge, it's hard to believe that the country music icon spent much of her upbringing inside its two rooms with her parents, Avie Lee and Robert Lee Parton, and her *ten* brothers and sisters (sadly, one of the Parton brothers, Larry, passed away only four days after his birth). The original home had no electricity or running water. Dolly says that even now her time in the cabin is dear to her heart, and she wrote a song in 1972, "My Tennessee Mountain Home," to express her feelings about it. Dolly's brother, Bobby Parton, built the replica in Dollywood, and their mother oversaw outfitting the interior so that it represented the original home as closely as possible.

The model rooms are set up as a combined living area and bedroom next to a kitchen with a wood-burning stove. Information plaques state that most of the pieces on display are real items taken from the real Sevierville, Tennessee, cabin. Try to spot things like cast iron cookware, handmade quilts, an old butter churn, straw broom, handmade furniture, and portraits of the Parton parents on the wall above the bed.

▶ *Park Pointers*

Winters in the Smoky Mountains can get quite cold. Dolly has told stories of what it was like growing up without electricity during the harsh-weather months. The interior walls of the cabin were covered in newspaper to provide additional insulation from the outside chill. The children slept fully dressed, several to a bed in the cabin's single bedroom, and weren't allowed to get up the next morning until their daddy built a fire to warm the rooms. The first time the Parton children—Dolly included—used a flush toilet was at an aunt's home in Knoxville. No one knew what to do with it, and they were afraid it was going to suck them right down! Though life in the mountains was bare-bones and provided only basic creature comforts—the children were always kept clothed and fed by their adoring mama—Dolly has shared nothing but warm memories of her childhood. Despite her undeniable success as a worldwide superstar, Dolly grew into a humble, kind, charismatic, and funny-as-heck person who is loved as much for her personality as for her talents.

Making Something Out of Nothing

Dolly always speaks affectionately of her dear mother, who worked hard to make sure her children felt cared for and loved. Special treats like fried chicken for special celebrations or banana puddin' made from discounted overripe bananas from a family friend's store make for fond memories of her family.

10. Dogs N Taters

FAST FACTS

WHAT: Freestanding quick-service lunch spot serving signature foot-long hot dogs, corn dogs, and crispy tater twirls.

WHERE: Quaint yellow and muted-green two-story cabin tucked into the back corner of Rivertown Junction.

EXPERT TIP: Line up your visit with a showtime at the Back Porch Theater right across the path. While roofed, the theater is outdoors, so it's no problem to grab a bench and enjoy your lunch from Dogs N Taters while watching the performers.

▶ Why You Should See It

Dogs N Taters is an underdog in the Dollywood food scene. Although the list of options is short and sweet—corn dogs, hot dogs, and the park's signature seasoned curly fries (tater twirls, to be exact)—they are all satisfyingly delicious! The charming walk-up stand is known for its fast service, so even if there's a line, it'll move quickly, and you won't have to wait too long to start noshing. Full-color photographs on the menu boards help with the decision-making process. A foot-long Nathan's hot dog (served in a matching extra-long bun) is the most classic choice and can be ordered plain or with chili and cheese. Or if you prefer your frank coated with thick buttermilk batter and deep-fried, you can get a little fancier with a corn dog breaded to crunchy perfection. The deep-fried tater twirls are a favorite among visitors and highly recommended. Super-crispy and seasoned just right, the piping-hot steamy potato curls are perfect as a lunch side dish or a snack all on their own. Dip them in ketchup or order them slathered in chili and melted cheese. Try them both ways and pick your favorite!

Dogs N Taters is located at a major intersection known as Village Pass, a wide walkway that connects two areas of the park. Walk toward the train tracks and make a right turn up the hill to access The Village and Country Fair or go left and you'll be at the base of Craftsman's Valley. This location is super convenient for grabbing a bite to eat while transitioning between areas to stave off any midday hunger.

▶ Park Pointers

Though the menu board only has combos listed—a duo of a hot dog or corn dog with tater twirls—you can order any item individually to make your snack even more portable. A crunchy corn dog on a stick is the perfect partner for trekking up the hill to The Village and hopping aboard the next Dollywood Express departure. Because the 'dogs are twice the length of a standard frank, order one to share and save money and extra room in your stomach for sampling other Dollywood treats. On your way out, don't forget to stop by the end of the counter to grab your favorite condiments and dipping sauces (probably a few napkins too) before continuing on your way.

A Varied Past

Prior to 2022, Village Pass was a pedestrian tunnel below the Inventor's Mansion, a fun house attraction that later became Rags to Riches, a museum celebrating Dolly that has since closed. The tunnel housed the Silver Dollar Arcade and a gemstone gift shop over the years, which were ultimately removed.

11. Smoky Mountain River Rampage

WHAT: White water rafting thrill ride with lap belt restraints. Riders must be at least 36 inches tall to hop on, and riders under 48 inches must be accompanied by a rider age 14 or older.

WHERE: Ride entrance is located just before the creek crossing to Jukebox Junction. Look for the boardwalk under a large plank sign.

EXPERT TIP: Don't bring anything that can be damaged by water onto the raft. Instead, use the lockers at the ride entrance to store your items for a fee or leave them with someone who isn't riding.

▶ Why You Should See It

Smoky Mountain River Rampage is one of Dollywood's most popular rides for cooling off on a hot day! The six-person rafts—really, they're more like giant bumper boats—move swiftly enough to kick up a breeze, but the ride isn't too scary for the younger members of your crew, making it a terrific family experience. The journey starts out slow and peaceful before a short rise followed by a mild drop and splash. Then you meander around some easy curves while enjoying the rocky scenery, complete with waterfalls, and encountering a few small white water drops that splash those with their backs toward them. A multistream waterfall passes by before the water speeds up into another short drop and a few foamy rapids. Things slow down after another short downhill plunge, and the raft passes a deserted blue rowboat on the shore before cruising under a tattered wooden bridge and then a second bridge where water cascading from above will give everyone a good soaking...or will it? The final mini thrill involves the raft rotating slowly—and suspensefully—while approaching a roaring waterfall. Will you be the one taking the hit, or will you be the one laughing at the unlucky ones who do? A ride on Smoky Mountain River Rampage is never the exact same every time, so a slightly different adventure awaits you each visit.

▶ Park Pointers

Don't ride if you don't want to get wet! In fact, after climbing aboard you'll probably have to sit in water droplets left behind from the previous ride. The rafts rotate naturally as they bob and weave their way down the river. There are a few sections with waterfalls, sprays, and splashes that'll soak riders on one side of the raft but not the other. Which side will you be on? There's no way to know! The constantly changing weight distribution in the rafts affects how much they rotate, so it's always a surprise to see who gets drenched and who gets merely sprinkled. Either way, you're guaranteed to have fun! Keep in mind that the attraction will close if there is lightning or heavy precipitation or if the outdoor temperature drops to 32°F (and won't open until temps climb above 40°F).

Line Up

This ride has one of the longest queues in Dollywood (don't worry, most of the waiting area is shaded), and it's even longer on hotter days. A little secret? Head for this ride if it starts to rain! The line tends to be shorter on an already wet day.

CHAPTER THREE

Jukebox Junction & The Dolly Parton Experience

Jukebox Junction is like walking through a time warp to 1950s Sevierville. Featuring vibrant facades and retro storefronts, it will immerse you in the world of Dolly's childhood. Enjoy a gentle ride in a vintage automobile or send your hair flying on a hot rod roller coaster. Finish up with a hamburger at an old-fashioned diner and with a themed live show to round out your visit.

The Dolly Parton Experience appeals to those who are Dolly Parton's biggest fans. From a walk-through of her luxury tour bus to an interactive experience telling the story of her journey from poor mountain girl to superstar, you'll get the full picture of Dolly's life. See actual pieces of Dolly's iconic style and get an up close look at the process of creating her custom looks, then round everything out with a live show featuring actual members of her family.

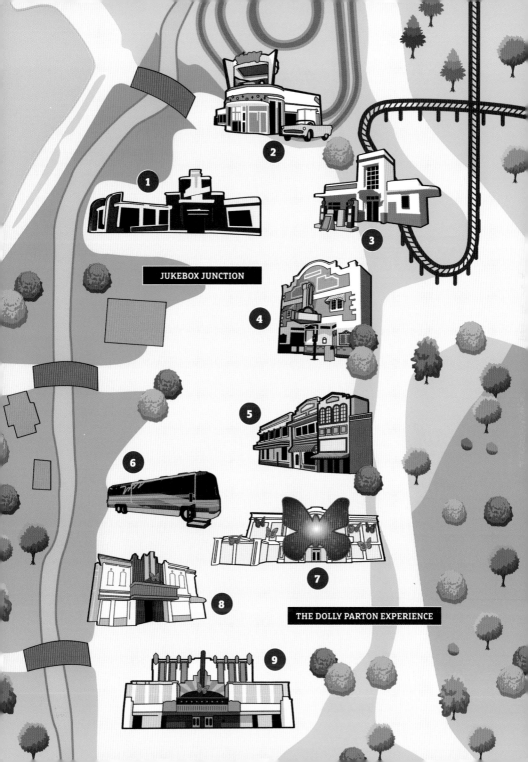

JUKEBOX JUNCTION

THE DOLLY PARTON EXPERIENCE

1. Red's Drive-In

WHAT: A classic American counter service restaurant known for delicious fries and old-fashioned hamburgers.

WHERE: Large retro-style building on the right-hand side as soon as you cross the bridge from Rivertown Junction.

EXPERT TIP: On a pretty day, choose one of the outdoor tables that overlook the creek behind the building to enjoy your meal. You may even spot some ducks waddling through!

▶ Why You Should See It

Back in 1946—the same year Dolly Parton was born—a small establishment called Red's Café opened in Sevierville. Dolly recalls eating her very first hamburger at Red's after a dentist appointment when she was a child. Paul "Red" Clevenger, the owner of the café, was known for his caring nature just as much as for his famous hamburgers. Red would often provide free food to families who needed to split a single meal between their children, showing that he cared more about his patrons than he did about his profits. With the 1995 opening of the Jukebox Junction area of the park, the essence of the original café was brought to life with Red's Drive-In, serving up crispy fries and juicy burgers with all the fixins'.

Walking into the bright red and silver building is like warping back to the 1950s. Take time to read the plaques accompanying the historical photos hanging on the walls. Take note of the authentic jukebox pumping out oldies tunes before you jump in line at the counter under the shiny retro metallic ceiling tiles to place your order. Red's main menu is simple but satisfying: mouthwatering burgers with or without cheese and bacon, and fries with or without chili and cheese. Turkey wraps and salads are also available, as well as a kids menu. Head over to the self-serve toppings and condiments bar to dress your burger just the way you like it. When you're ready to grab a seat, don't worry, because Red's has plenty! Booths and tables are available inside if you need respite from the weather, and there is also ample space outdoors, both covered and open-air.

▶ Park Pointers

If you've been to Dollywood before, you're probably wondering: Where are the milkshakes?! It's true that Red's used to serve thick and creamy milkshakes in fun flavors like creamsicle and Fruity Pebbles. In recent seasons, however, the milkshakes disappeared from the menu and have yet to return. There's been no official announcement of when or if folks will be able to get their shake fix again at Red's (or why the milkshakes were removed from the menu in the first place), but until then, fans hold out hope! Soda lovers, you're in luck, however! Coca-Cola Freestyle machines are available at Red's so you can mix and match your perfect fizzy flavor. Red's is located directly across from two of Dollywood's popular attractions: Rockin' Roadway and Lightning Rod. Both can have lengthy wait times, so planning to grab a snack or a quick lunch between rides can break up the boredom of standing in line.

Recharge

Each stool at the long counters inside Red's has a USB port for fueling up your phone while you fuel up your body. Outside, look for the charging stations disguised as giant red Coca-Cola bottles near the seating areas.

2. Rockin' Roadway

FAST FACTS

WHAT: A slow two-person track ride in self-driving classic cars. Uses lap belt restraints. No minimum height requirement, though riders under 42 inches tall must be accompanied by someone age 14 or older.

WHERE: Corner building styled like a retro service station across from Red's Drive-In, with spray-painted windows and a retro police car parked out front.

EXPERT TIP: The queue area is indoors and climate-controlled, so the wait is comfortable on more crowded days.

▶ Why You Should See It

There's a reason many folks will name Rockin' Roadway as their favorite Dollywood ride despite it lacking the adrenaline rush of, say, the Lightning Rod coaster right next door. Rockin' Roadway is themed to the max and promises enjoyment for the entire family, from the very young to the young at heart. The ride queue begins when you step through the glass doors of the vintage service station. The front room contains switchbacks that eventually lead to a high-ceilinged garage area where the line continues up a flight of stairs. On the platform at the top, the line splits into two sections, each leading down a staircase to the boarding area. The ride is the same regardless of which section you choose, so hop into the one that is shortest (of course). When it's your turn to board, up to two riders will step into a miniaturized version of a classic car. You may get a Thunderbird, Corvette, or Cadillac in pink, white, yellow, green, or blue. Unfortunately, you can't pick your car, but that's okay: They're all really cool. Then you're off! The car mostly guides itself along the rail in the center of the track, though whoever is sitting in the driver's seat has some control using the loose steering wheel. There's also a button to honk the horn, so don't forget to blare it as often as you wish. Enjoy the retro scenery of car sales lots with vehicles similar to the one you're riding, colorful pennant streamers, and mid-century advertisements. At the end of the track your car returns to the garage, where you disembark and exit up the stairs to the right. Rockin' Roadway is a pleasant ride that lets you sit back and relax in the middle of a bustling day.

▶ Park Pointers

If you're a Dollywood regular, get into the habit of snapping a selfie from inside the car each time you ride. Before long, you'll have an awesome collection of similar yet slightly varying images. This can be an especially sentimental habit if you're always riding with the same person! When planning your trip, keep in mind that Rockin' Roadway will close during certain inclement weather conditions, especially lightning or extreme precipitation. The cars are all convertibles and open to the air, so you may be exposed to the sun or light rain or snow for the duration of your ride. If someone in your group is too short to see over the steering wheel, a cushioned booster seat will be provided as soon as you board.

The Real Deal

Did you notice that the mocked-up service station housing Rockin' Roadway is named Watson Motor Company? The name is a throwback to a real business in Sevierville. Dolly recalls looking at all the cars parked on the Watson lot when her family—who didn't own a vehicle—went into town.

3. Lightning Rod

WHAT: Hybrid wood and steel high-thrills roller coaster. Riders must be at least 48 inches tall. Guests with casts above the elbow or any hard casts on legs are not allowed to ride.

WHERE: You can't miss this massive coaster towering above Jukebox Junction. The entrance is situated between Pines Theater and Rockin' Roadway.

EXPERT TIP: Once you've conquered the coaster, head across to the corner store, Hi-Octane Ride Souvenirs, for some exclusive Lightning Rod merch.

▶ Why You Should See It

Arguably Dollywood's "scariest" coaster, reaching speeds of 73 mph and sending riders down a knuckle-clenching 165-foot plunge, Lightning Rod is for thrill seekers only! While whizzing along the 3,800-foot track, you'll feel yourself lift off the seat for almost twenty total seconds of airtime! The coaster train seats two per row and is modeled and painted to look like a 1950s hot rod. Entering the queue, you pass old-timey gas pumps and then find yourself in (fictional) hot rod mechanic Johnny Rev's garage. Trophies and design schematics offer clues about the story of Johnny's craving for inventing vehicles that test the limits of speed. When you reach the third floor of the garage, you realize that you'll be taking a test ride in "Lightning Rod," Johnny Rev's newest creation. After climbing into the seat and leaving the garage, you turn a curve before suddenly accelerating via a super-speed chain lift up a massive hill. From there, you plunge down a set of twin drops before rocketing down the ride's longest and steepest drop. If you're not windblown enough by now, near the end you encounter one of the ride's most daring features: a series of four consecutive drops that leave your stomach somewhere on the hill above. Your heart is sure to be *thump-thumping* by the time you climb back onto the loading platform. The ride is short at just over one minute before the brake run. Enjoy your bragging rights after having the guts to conquer this beast!

▶ *Park Pointers*

When the $22 million ride opened in 2016, it was the fastest wooden roller coaster in the world as well as the first launched wooden coaster. After experiencing repeated downtimes due to technical difficulties with the special launch system and excess stress on portions of the track, the ride was closed for the final portion of an already shortened 2020 season to undergo some major changes. Portions of the wooden track were replaced with steel I-Box track, making Lightning Rod a true hybrid coaster. In 2023, the ride was closed again to replace the original launch mechanism with a high-speed chain lift. Certain weather conditions will cause the ride to close, including heavy rain, snow, ice, lightning, high winds, or a temperature of 36°F or lower. Use Dollywood's mobile app to keep tabs on the wait time (and possible downtime!) while in the park, especially if you plan on riding more than once!

 One of the Best

> In 2022, *USA TODAY* named Lightning Rod one of the top 10 best roller coasters in the country!

4. Pines Theater

FAST FACTS

WHAT: Classic mid-century indoor theater featuring live performances of famous hits from times gone by.

WHERE: At the end of Jukebox Junction's Main Street. Look for the faux old-timey box office and flashing lights!

EXPERT TIP: Have a full retro-themed date night by grabbing a burger at Red's Drive-In, taking a spin on the Rockin' Roadway, and finishing up with a show at the Pines. Poodle skirts optional.

▶ Why You Should See It

Pines Theater is a throwback to a former 700-seat movie theater and live entertainment venue in Sevierville. In 1944, the original Pines Theater opened for the first time and hosted many concerts and films during the following years. Later, in 1956, a 10-year-old Dolly Parton had her first paid performance at the Pines when she appeared on the *Cas Walker Farm and Home Tour* variety show. Dollywood's version of Pines Theater—complete with its brilliant marquee—combines Dolly's cherished memories of 1950s Sevierville with her lifelong love of musical performance.

Pines rotates through a variety of shows, though those with a retro flair bolster the theme of Jukebox Junction with high-energy performances featuring poodle skirts, saddle shoes, and slicked-back hair. The popular *Dreamland Drive-In* spectacular fills a frequent spot on the theater's schedule and is a musical journey through the biggest hits from the 1950s and 1960s with dazzling decade-appropriate costumes and colorful sets. As the seasons change, so do the shows, giving you something new to check out at Dollywood all year long. You might catch a water-themed summer musical featuring hits like "Splish Splash" and "Singin' in the Rain," or a holiday retelling of "'Twas the Night Before Christmas." There's not a bad seat in the comfortable indoor auditorium, so carve out a spot in your day for this nostalgic attraction. Before grabbing a seat to see the show, stop by Pines Theater Concessions for necessary theater snacks like popcorn, cotton candy, butterfly pretzels, and more!

▶ Park Pointers

While the original Pines Theater in Sevierville is no more, the Pines building itself is still standing and can be found at the corner of Court Avenue and Joy Street. In 2022, the building underwent a major renovation when The Pines Downtown—an entertainment lounge and event venue—opened, evoking a mood that pays homage to the building's musical roots as well as attracts a modern crowd. A new marquee was installed that is reminiscent of the original theater's entrance. On the broad side of the building, a mural was painted by artist Seth Bishop depicting the theater's most famous performers: Chet Akins, June Carter Cash, Archie Campbell, Roy Acuff, and of course a young Dolly Parton! Dolly was especially excited about the new lounge offering games—like duckpin bowling, giant Jenga, and a retro gaming cocktail corner—because she remembers variety show host Cas Walker coming up with fun things for folks to experience in addition to the performances to fill the seats in the original theater.

Dolly & June Carter Cash

Dolly and June Carter Cash performed on the same evenings at the original Pines Theater following June's divorce from Carl Smith. The two appeared together later on the Grand Ole Opry and recalled fond memories of their performances together.

5. Storefronts with Stories

WHAT: Faux businesses and storefronts that hold clues about Dolly Parton's history.

WHERE: Peppered along the street in Jukebox Junction. If you can't open the door, you've probably found one.

EXPERT TIP: Find them all and drop some Dollywood knowledge on the people in your group!

▶ Why You Should See It

When you cross into Jukebox Junction, you feel like you have stepped into a time machine and been whisked back to mid-century East Tennessee. The paths of the park are transformed into roads with pavement markings running alongside sidewalks with vintage streetlamps overhead. While the area is chock-full of things to do as far as dining, shopping, and theme park attraction riding, there's also quite a bit of hidden history seamlessly integrated into the theme. As you browse Main Street—the road winding through the center of Jukebox Junction—notice the shops that appear to be locked or closed. There you'll find tributes to some folks who were influential in Dolly's life and career.

One such storefront is Cas Walker's Super Market, with its green-striped awning, double doors, and bay windows advertising the day's offerings. Check out the harvest baskets full of fruits and vegetables seen through a window—and take note of those prices! Wow! Cas Walker is the person who helped Dolly launch her career starting when she was only 10 years old. She performed on the TV and radio shows he hosted in an effort to promote his chain of grocery stores in Knoxville as well as some locations in Kentucky and Virginia.

Continue down the street and you'll come across Judy's Luggage & Millinery. The window display shows travel-related items such as maps, globes, and suitcases. The store's name references Dolly's childhood best friend, Judy Ogle, who has collaborated with Dolly on many projects throughout her career (even to this day!), including managing wardrobe on film sets and traveling with Dolly...hence the title of the faux shop!

The third mock-up shop is a nod to a man who served as Dollywood's vice president of maintenance and construction, Howard Decaussin. The shop—aptly named Howard's TV Repair—displays vintage TV sets and lettering promising services of installed antennas, new and rebuilt TVs, and parts. Following the death of the real Howard in 1995 (which was also the year Jukebox Junction opened), Dolly wrote a song about him for his late wife (called "Widow"), further exemplifying how much Dolly appreciated his presence in her life.

▶ Park Pointers

This area is full of other fun hidden details that flesh out the retro theme, so try to take them all in when passing through. Look up, down, and around while strolling the streets. A couple of faux fronts may even make you giggle, like Dr. Kane U. Seagoode's optometry clinic. On peak attendance days at Dollywood, the streets of Jukebox Junction down through The Dolly Parton Experience can feel a bit less crowded and more peaceful than other areas of the park. Take your time strolling through the area and taking in the stories of Dolly's childhood and history as an actress, singer, songwriter, and theme park tycoon.

6. Dolly's Home-on-Wheels

WHAT: Dolly Parton's retired tour bus parked permanently in Dollywood and open for park visitors to explore.

WHERE: Parked on the campus of the brand-new Dolly Parton Experience.

EXPERT TIP: To keep the bus in pristine condition, this attraction may close during extreme weather conditions.

▶ Why You Should See It

Dolly's luxurious $750,000 tour bus—in use from the mid-nineties to the early twenty-first century—moved to its new permanent location in the former Adventures in Imagination area in 2009 following the retirement of the 1994 Prevost motor coach. When Adventures in Imagination was reimagined into The Dolly Parton Experience in 2024, the bus remained a prominent attraction. It's a well-known fact that Dolly has a strong dislike for flying and prefers the comfort of her personal tour bus to hotel rooms while traveling, so she kept to the road as much as possible. The inside of the RV was outfitted specifically for Dolly's practical needs and those of the ones who traveled with her. Living up to the name of the attraction, the bus really is a perfect 45-foot-long home on wheels.

After climbing into the vehicle and passing the driver's seat, you'll find yourself in the living and kitchen area of the bus. A comfortable leather couch sits across from a matching dinette adjacent to the kitchen counter complete with sink, storage cabinets, overhead microwave, and refrigerator with freezer. The middle section of the coach houses triple bunk beds with the top two sporting personalized pillows embroidered with the names Judy (Dolly's childhood best friend) and Don, her longtime manager, driver, and friend. Across from the bunks are two back-to-back half baths, one exclusively for Dolly, and the entire back of the bus contains Dolly's shower, vanity, and bedroom. Looking as if Dolly herself just stepped outside and headed for the stage, the vanity is complete with pink cosmetic case and makeup brushes. The bedroom features plush paisley bedding with personal framed photos along the dresser top, a guitar, and several of Dolly's stage outfits and accessories can be found tucked into the closet. Only a small group of people are allowed in the bus at one time, so you may have to wait a few minutes to board, but the line tends to move quickly as visitors go in and out of Dolly's mobile abode.

▶ Park Pointers

There's one name you'll see repeated on and around Dolly's Home-On-Wheels: Don Warden. From the star on the sidewalk proclaiming him as "Dolly's #1 Angel" to the plaque outside of the door describing him as a mentor, musician, manager, and Mr. Everything, Don was someone very dear to Dolly's life who did "a little bit of everything" for her career. An original member of the Porter Wagoner Trio and Steel Guitar Hall of Fame member, Don met Dolly when she joined "The Porter Wagoner Show" in 1967. After Parton left the show in 1974, Don went with her and began his many decades as her bus driver, mechanic, show promoter, merchandise coordinator, and so much more. He and his wife, Ann, are credited with the interior design of Dolly's Home-On-Wheels. Following his passing in 2017, Dolly stated that a piece of her heart and a huge piece of her life is now missing.

7. Songteller

WHAT: A self-guided, immersive exhibit that will take you on the journey of Dolly's upbringing from poor country girl to international superstar.

WHERE: Three words: "massive pink butterfly."

EXPERT TIP: Get up close to the big butterfly on the building for a surprise! The pink sparkles are actually an illusion created from hundreds of free-hanging sections that flutter in the breeze.

▶ Why You Should See It

If you have been visiting Dollywood for years, the first thing you'll notice when walking into the plaza of The Dolly Parton Experience following the spring 2024 renovations is the Songteller building. The facade is truly a stunning sight. The glittering wings of the massive pink butterfly (the universal symbol of Dolly) are hard to miss. Inside, Songteller adds a modern, digital dimension to presenting Dolly's heartwarming story. Themed vignettes of poignant moments during her climb to the top feature actual props and costumes and vintage footage of a young Dolly doing what she does best. One room of the building is designed to resemble a commuter bus, where visitors can sit in the faux bus seats, with luggage in the racks overhead, and watch a video chronicling Dolly's journey to Nashville. These unique setups provide an intimate glimpse into Dolly's storied past.

The centerpiece of Songteller is undoubtedly the 360-degree projection room. This enveloping experience features Dolly herself narrating her move to Nashville and her rise in the country music industry. The room's design allows visitors to feel as though they are part of the story, surrounded by vivid projections that re-create significant moments from Dolly's career. It's an exhilarating show that lets fans feel what it's like to be onstage experiencing the energy and excitement of performing in front of thousands of people. Songteller is a must-see for any Dolly Parton fan, combining emotional storytelling with cool technology that'll bring a tear to your eye and warmth to your heart.

▶ Park Pointers

The Songteller building was originally built in the 1950s and opened as the Silver Screen Café, a restaurant with dishes named after blockbuster film titles. The restaurant was only open for one season before being reimagined as a deli-style establishment called DJ Platters until 2002. Then, up until 2024, the building was home to the Chasing Rainbows Museum. The museum was an earlier version of Songteller. On display were artifacts from Dolly's life, including her high school band uniform, her and her husband's wedding clothes, many historical photographs, and more. Guests wound their way through the multistory attraction while listening to Dolly's music and learning about her journey from living at home with her family to living life as an international superstar.

New Attraction, New Dolly!

In November 2023, Dolly released her forty-nineth solo studio album, Rockstar. Her newest project is a collection of twenty-one rock covers and collaborations and nine original songs—her first foray into the rock genre. The album was inspired by her 2022 induction into the Rock & Roll Hall of Fame that she initially declined, stating she had not yet earned it.

8. Behind the Seams

═══ FAST FACTS ═══

WHAT: From Dolly's earliest days onstage to her most recent ventures, this colorful exhibit is all about her most visible asset: her iconic look!

WHERE: Look for an elaborate pink and gold facade with scripty lettering on the building next to Dolly's tour bus.

EXPERT TIP: Pick up a full-color hardback copy of *Behind the Seams: My Life in Rhinestones*—available at the Dollywood Emporium and Dolly's Fan Shop—and take home the story of Dolly's style.

▶ Why You Should See It

Dolly has always said that her songwriting is what is most important to her, but she also looks amazing while doing it! Behind the Seams is fully dedicated to Dolly's fashion, with a special focus on the substantial amount of work that goes into getting her ready for the spotlight. Dolly insists on showing up fashion-appropriate for every occasion, be it a performance, an awards ceremony, or the opening of a new attraction at Dollywood. Always a jokester, she likes to say it takes a lot of money to look cheap! In this exhibit, you can get up close and personal with where all that money goes. See Dolly's actual custom costumes, wigs, accessories, and shoes. At 78 years old, the 5-foot, 0-inch singer is still rocking stiletto heels that many people decades younger wouldn't dare wear. Never before have you been able to take in all the tiny details that come together to create Dolly's unforgettable look, which has kept people talkin' and gossipin' since the beginning of her career.

While most of the exhibit keeps Dolly's possessions safely behind glass, there are a couple of interactive elements that allow you to touch and feel. You can take a seat at a brightly lit vanity, tucked away in a corner, that's similar to one Dolly would use to get ready for a public appearance. Surrounding the vanity are some amazing vintage photos of Dolly sitting at similar desks while getting ready for an event. At the Dress Up Dolly wall, you can be a kid again and play with oversized magnetic paper dolls of Dolly! Choose combinations of costumes, wigs, and accessories to create your favorite Parton ensemble.

▶ *Park Pointers*

Before the opening of The Dolly Parton Experience in May 2024, the building that is now home to Behind the Seams was another style-centric setup called Dolly's Closet. The specialized boutique sold clothing and accessories that aligned with Dolly's personal style, including both casual and formal attire. Dolly Parton's real wardrobe has been coordinated by stylist Steve Summers for more than three decades. It's no secret that Dolly loves bright colors and all the glitz and glam she can pack into a single outfit, and Summers is the man who makes that happen. Starting as a performer in Dollywood and eventually as one of Dolly's onstage dance partners, Summers began making suggestions about the costumes used in the shows. The rest, as they say, is history. Whatever the occasion, Summers is there to make sure Dolly is dressed just right to suit both the theme of the event and her personal flair for style.

Dedicated to Fashion

On Dolly's lavish property just outside Nashville, Tennessee, there is a guesthouse used solely for designing and planning her clothing and accessories. The rooms within contain sewing machines, design boards, organized closets, and custom-built mannequins sized to Parton's precise measurements.

9. DreamSong Theater and Precious Memories

═══ **FAST FACTS** ═══

WHAT: A five hundred–seat indoor theater with Dolly's own family members performing musical extravaganzas.

WHERE: Large cream and purple building facing the thoroughfare of The Dolly Parton Experience.

EXPERT TIP: Pay close attention to the screen behind the stage. How many important figures from Dolly's life can you recognize in the slideshow?

▶ Why You Should See It

DreamSong Theater is a sentimental place for Dolly. It is a musical venue that is home to live performances with a cast of some of Dolly's own relatives. What better way to add a personal touch to a Dollywood show than to make it a family production? The cushy air-conditioned space features stadium-style seating with upholstered chairs, drink holders, and clear views of the multiplatform stage. When the theater was unveiled in 2013, the first production was *My People*, with Parton siblings, nieces, and cousins filling out the list of performers. The show depicted the life story of a little girl just like Dolly—a Southern gal with a big family and big dreams—beating the odds and achieving huge success. The theater continues its tradition of including Dolly's family members in its cast of characters with performances of *Harmonies of the Heart*. An exploration of the star's history, *Harmonies of the Heart* is a spin-off of a 2020 Dollywood Christmas show, *Heart of the Holidays*. Two of Dolly's nieces star in the show, singing a mix of Dolly's hits and original songs, while also sharing sweet memories of their dear aunt against a backdrop of photographs and video clips of her early life and mountain upbringing. In 2024, a brand-new show starring Dolly's niece Heidi Parton was added at the theater. *Heidi Parton Kin & Friends* was written by both Heidi and Dolly and includes songs that have personal significance for their family.

Precious Memories is an exhibit added to the lobby of the updated theater. The walls of this new display are covered with monitors designed to look like windows that offer a peek into Dolly's past. The slideshows focus on Dolly's family, her faith, and what has inspired her through the years. When Dolly first saw the exhibit for herself, she had a strong emotional reaction, more so than any of the other new attractions in The Dolly Parton Experience.

▶ *Park Pointers*

Prior to 2013, the building that is home to the current DreamSong Theater was known as Imagination Cinema, specializing in simulator rides and multidimensional experiences. Thunder Road—renamed White Lightnin' in 2009—was one such attraction: a ride that debuted in 1996 and featured seats that moved along with a film depicting moonshine shenanigans and a high-energy car chase. The building was also home to seasonal presentations such as *The Polar Express 4D*, *Cloudy with a Chance of Meatballs 4D*, and *Journey to the Center of the Earth 4D*. Needless to say, the building has had many roles in Dollywood's history before settling into the comfort zone of a beautiful family theater. DreamSong Theater is also where Dollywood's Calming Room—a special haven for guests with special needs—can be found. The room features a teepee, beanbag chairs, weighted blankets, and dimmable lights. It can be reserved via the Ride Accessibility Center on Showstreet.

CHAPTER FOUR

Country Fair

★

Reminiscent of the midway of classic county fairs, Country Fair is all about rides, rides, rides! Here, you'll find all the classic favorites and discover some new ones as well. You can be heck on wheels in bumper cars, scramble your equilibrium on rides that whirl and twirl, or defy gravity by flying high into the air. If your stomach is up for it, follow up afterward with some fried chicken tenders, crispy fries, and a cone swirled high with soft serve before attempting to win the biggest prize in a selection of old-fashioned carnival games. If it's fun you're after, you'll find it here!

COUNTRY FAIR

1. Carnival Games

WHAT: A collection of old-fashioned carnival games that let you try your hand at winning prizes!

WHERE: On both sides of the path when entering Country Fair, down the hill from The Village.

EXPERT TIP: Use a light hand for tossing games for a better chance at a win. Less force = better aim!

▶ Why You Should See It

Walking through the games section of Country Fair will take you right back to visiting county and state fairs past and present. Colorful plush prizes hang from the game booths, enticing you to come over and take a chance at getting to go home with one of the little (or giant) cuties. Prizes change depending on the season and current trends, so there's always something new to go after. Unlike most of the other attractions in Dollywood, you will need to purchase special vouchers in order to play the carnival games. Vouchers can be obtained at the kiosk located near the games area, and you can take advantage of quantity discounts to get up to five free vouchers (see the kiosk host for the most updated pricing info). Unused vouchers do not roll over into the next season, so use them or lose them!

Games you can play are many and varied, but each one boasts an exciting challenge to test your skills. Goblet Toss will have you tossing pickleballs at an array of goblets, aiming for the few colored containers that will land you a prize. The water gun race will arm you with water pistols to shoot at a target in an effort to fill a tube with colored lights—first one to fill the tube wins! The "derby" game is best described as a cross between a horse race, arcade Skee-Ball, and golf. Players roll golf balls up a short alley, aiming for holes that affect the speed of the horses making their way across the track. Whether you're a sharpshooter or just in it for laughs, this corner of Dollywood is a place where everyone's a winner in the game of enjoyment.

▶ *Park Pointers*

The ring toss is known as one of the hardest games to win—though it also awards the largest prizes—so if your goal is to take home any prize at all, you might want to avoid that one! If you want to ensure your family wins something, choose a game where you are competing against other players, like the water gun race. Wait until your group is the only one waiting to play; that way someone in the group will definitely come out on top! Keep in mind, however, that Package Pickup is not available for game prizes, so be prepared to cart around whatever swag you score for the rest of your visit.

More Games!

There is an area with similar carnival games at the very end of Wilderness Pass where the path takes a turn at the Tennessee Tornado coaster in Craftsman's Valley. Try both locations! Vouchers can be purchased at both.

2. The Waltzing Swinger

═══ FAST FACTS ═══

WHAT: Chair swing ride with lap bar and between-the-leg restraints. Riders must be at least 42 inches tall, and those under 48 inches must be accompanied by someone age 14 or older.

WHERE: Tucked into the bottom corner of Country Fair, across from The Scrambler and right next to the Celebration Hall picnic pavilion.

EXPERT TIP: Choose one of the seats in the outer ring to experience the most force.

▶ Why You Should See It

Undeniably one of the most beautifully decorated rides in Country Fair, The Waltzing Swinger is a classic carnival staple that sends riders on a gravity-defying ride that twirls high above the paths below. Before boarding, take a moment to appreciate the colorful city scenes painted on the ovals both inside and on the outer rim of the carousel-like canopy. After making it through the outdoor queue, grab a seat in one of the red bucket chairs hanging from four metal chains that attach each chair to the canopy. The chairs are mostly for single riders, though several double chairs are available for those who don't meet the solo rider height requirement, or who need a hand to hold on this semi-intense ride. Once you're buckled in, the ride starts out slow and gentle as the "swings" slowly rise from the ground. The velocity quickly increases and things get exciting as the canopy starts to tilt in one direction, then another, and the swings swirl around from the increasing centripetal force. The total ride is about a minute-and-a-half long, and you'll be feeling the wind in your hair for most of that time. Chair swing rides toe the line between mild and moderate thrills and are a great "gateway" ride for younger guests who want to start experimenting with grown-up rides! Wait time for this ride isn't usually long, so it's one you can hop on easily while exploring the Fair.

▶ Park Pointers

This attraction was originally a different chair swing that was known as Swingamajig. The older ride was simpler in design and had fewer swings. A Waveswinger ride, it was built by Chance Rides in the US. It opened in 1980, a ghost of the pre-Dollywood days when the park was called Silver Dollar City. After the attraction was closed and removed in 2004, The Waltzing Swinger was born, this one also a Waveswinger but built by Italian manufacturer Sartori. Certain extreme weather conditions will cause this ride to close, including temperatures dropping to 23°F or below, extreme precipitation, high winds, or lightning within 10 miles of the park.

3. The Scrambler

WHAT: Old-fashioned scrambler ride with lap bar restraints. Riders must be 36 inches tall to ride, and those under 48 inches must be accompanied by someone age 14 or older.

WHERE: Red, yellow, and silver structure located across from the Grandstand Café in Country Fair. If it's spinning and twisting and twirling all at the same time, you've found it.

EXPERT TIP: To reduce dizziness, keep your eyes focused on a point in front of you inside your car.

▶ Why You Should See It

If you've ever wondered what it feels like to be inside an eggbeater, ride The Scrambler! Those prone to experiencing motion sickness should give this one a wide berth, because you're gonna be zipping and twirling and swirling from any and all directions. Each carriage seats one to three people—depending how many fit comfortably—and the seats are clustered in sets of four. The ride starts slowly, each cluster spinning around while, at the same time, all the clusters rotate around the ride's center axis. As the speed picks up, you're whipped from side to side in your seat—you may even get pushed right into your friends—and it gets hard to keep track of just exactly where you are! Over here? Over there? Everywhere? The best way to ride is to relax your body and give in to the motion instead of fighting against it. The movements will feel smoother that way! After almost two minutes of scramblin', you finally slow to a stop. From there, your final challenge is trying to walk in a straight line to find the exit! This has been a beloved attraction at Dollywood for over thirty years and is worth a ride.

▶ Park Pointers

Scrambler rides were invented by a Georgia man named Richard Harris. The first of his scramblers was installed at Lakewood Fairgrounds in Atlanta, Georgia, in 1938. Three years later, Harris was granted a US design patent, which was then licensed to the Eli Bridge Company, the manufacturer of most of the scramblers in existence today—including the one at Dollywood! The Scrambler is one of Country Fair's original rides when the Fair opened to visitors in 1993. When designing the nostalgic area, Dolly called up memories of visiting the midway at the county fair when she was a child. The Scrambler will close when there is heavy rain, snow, or ice, as well as when lightning strikes are detected within 5 miles of the park.

4. Demolition Derby

═══ FAST FACTS ═══

WHAT: A classic theme park favorite: bumper cars! Low-thrills family ride with lap bar restraints. Must be at least 42 inches tall to ride and at least 48 inches tall to drive.

WHERE: Covered structure in the heart of Country Fair. Listen for the bumps, bangs, and squeals of fun coming from riders within.

EXPERT TIP: If you don't want to get hit, keep your car close to the outer walls to avoid the major traffic jams that happen in the center.

▶ Why You Should See It

This ride is quintessential theme park fun! What's a fair without bumper cars? Almost anything goes when you climb behind the wheel of a two-seater brightly colored car with a 360-degree rubber bumper. Once the ride attendant has made the rounds and checked that all lap bars are locked down, the chase is on! Drivers and riders move along the enclosed arena in a counterclockwise direction with questionable control over their cars. What happens during the two-minute ride is up to you...mostly. Will you chase down the other drivers and bump as many cars as possible while cackling maniacally? Will you be a responsible driver and meander around the circle at low speed, avoiding conflict at all cost? The choice is yours, but don't forget everyone else gets that choice, too, so keep your eyes open, check those blind spots, and try not to get hit! If things get too crazy or jammed up, the ride pauses while the attendant gives instructions over the loudspeaker on how to break things up. Problems typically occur when someone accidentally turns their car around and starts heading the wrong way...driving on the wrong side of the road would put a wrench in your commute any day, for sure!

▶ Park Pointers

The Demolition Derby arena and most of the queue area are covered, making the ride a good choice for days when it's drizzling or flurrying. If lightning strikes too close to the park grounds, however, the cars will stop operations temporarily until the storm moves along. While the ride is family safe, getting bashed into unexpectedly can result in sudden jerks, scoots, or spins. Those with certain health conditions or with problems with their neck or back will want to use caution before deciding to ride. Read the safety rules on the wooden board posted at the beginning of the line for the most up-to-date information. Bumper car–like rides have been around since the 1920s, but did you know that the original point of these rides was to *avoid* other cars? Initially called dodgems, the early versions of these rides would result in drivers being asked to leave if they bumped into other cars. Eventually, it became clear that the real fun lay in slamming into as many cars as possible, and the modern-day bumper car ride was born!

Real-Life Bumper Cars

After Dolly bought her first brand-new car once she started making big money, she drove to her first studio session at RCA and accidentally slammed into the side of their newest building when she failed to brake on time. Not wanting to be late, she just got out, left the car there, and went inside to sing!

5. Happy Valley Farmyard

WHAT: A trio of adorable animal-themed rides perfect for the youngest Dollywood visitors. Uses cloth seat belt restraints and has no minimum height requirement. Children may ride alone.

WHERE: The trio of rides have their own little section nestled at the bottom of Country Fair.

EXPERT TIP: Grab some snacks, settle in, and let the kiddos ride several times over. You deserve the break!

▶ Why You Should See It

These charming mini roundabouts are the only rides in Dollywood with no minimum height restriction or requirement to ride with an older partner, so bring your littlest kiddos on over to this nook of Country Fair and let them ride to their heart's content! Choose between oversized yellow ducks, friendly bumblebees, or smiling pink piggies, and enjoy some very-not-scary Dollywood experiences. All three rides are covered, offering shade on hot days and shelter during light rainfall.

Lucky Ducky and Piggy Parade are basic go-around-in-a-circle rides, with carts for Lucky Ducky shaped like sly side-glancing ducks wearing colorful shirts and for Piggy Parade like cute, chubby pink piggies. Each cart has two rows of seats, and an adult can sit in the back row if they want to ride along as well. If you choose to wait outside while your child rides, you can enter the ride at the beginning and end of the cycle to help buckle and unbuckle the lap restraint. The rides do not spin quickly and shouldn't be too intense or dizzying, making them perfect for tiny Dollywood recruits!

Last but certainly not least is Busy Bees, the most "daring" of the three rides and a young fan favorite. Riders climb inside doe-eyed bumblebees and get extra secured with a strap that goes across the shoulder (like the seat belt on a car). The bees rotate slowly around a big yellow beehive, and there is a button next to the nonfunctional steering wheel that will make the bee go up and down—but not too high—giving riders a bit of extra excitement. Fair warning: The theme song that plays nonstop over the loudspeaker will get stuck in your head for the rest of the day.

▶ Park Pointers

These kid-centric rides started operating in 2005 and have been serving up smiles for almost two decades. For a slightly different experience, make a stop at these rides at night to watch them come alive with lights. Busy Bees, Piggy Parade, and Lucky Ducky will close when lightning has been detected within 5 miles of the park. These rides may also close during other extreme weather conditions, such as heavy rain, snow, or hail.

6. Grandstand Café

FAST FACTS

WHAT: Casual lunch spot serving hot dogs, fries, simple salads, chicken tenders, and kids meals.

WHERE: Centrally located in Country Fair behind The Scrambler.

EXPERT TIP: Send a member of your group to scout out an empty picnic table while you wait in line.

▶ Why You Should See It

In Country Fair, Grandstand Café is the best place to fuel up while working your way through all the rides in the area. Inside the covered counter service stand, you can find hot lunch items like crispy seasoned chicken tenders, hot dogs in toasted buns (with or without chili and cheese), crinkle fries, Caesar salads, and vegan garden salads. Vegan hot dogs are available as well! Dollywood is great about catering to kids with meals familiar to them, so you can also find peanut butter and jelly sandwiches or kids hot dogs served with applesauce, animal crackers, and choice of beverage. Though Grandstand isn't a dedicated sweets location, you can purchase soft chocolate chip cookies and fudgy brownies to get your sugar fix. The original menu at Grandstand included one of Dollywood's award-winning dishes—Frannie's Famous Fried Chicken Sandwich—featuring pickle-brined fried chicken with a crispy breading that had the tiniest hint of sweetness. The sandwich has been missing from Dollywood menus in recent years, but it lives on in the memories of longtime park goers.

▶ *Park Pointers*

Across from Grandstand Café is a large grassy picnic area with tables under umbrellas ideal for stopping to rest and have a snack. Back in 2005, this was the site of a kid-friendly coaster called VeggieTales Sideshow Spin, themed after the popular children's show at the time. Later, in 2012, the ride removed the VeggieTales motif, the track was repainted green and peach, and the name was shortened to Sideshow Spin. After the 2016 season, the ride was removed and relocated to Kentucky Shores Family Fun Center, where it was known as Veggie Tale Spin, but was soon closed down and sent overseas to London after the ground was determined to be too soft to safely support it. Now the site is an expansion of the outdoor seating available near Grandstand.

Don't Forget Dessert

After finishing your lunch at Grandstand Café, head just around the corner to Blue Ribbon Cones for a classic swirly soft-serve ice cream cone or an old-fashioned soda float! For a treat that's extra special, ask for a chocolate-dipped cone with nuts or sprinkles.

7. Lemon Twist

WHAT: Spinning teacup ride with bench seats and no restraints. No minimum height requirement, though riders under 48 inches tall must be accompanied by someone age 14 or older.

WHERE: Against the tree line on the Southern side of Country Fair.

EXPERT TIP: To lessen dizziness, ride with people who agree to a "no spin" plan where no one is allowed to touch the wheel in the center of the teacup!

▶ Why You Should See It

Dollywood's take on the classic teacups ride, Lemon Twist is for those who love to spin, spin, and spin some more! Line up underneath the cheery citrus-yellow and royal blue canopies and wait to board the oversized teacups, each sitting on its own saucer. A circular bench inside the teacup can seat however many people can fit comfortably. A seat gate will be closed and latched by the ride attendant, securing you and your riding partners in the teacup. Then it's time to get moving! The teacups are dispersed among three rotating circular platforms, while the larger striped turntable that contains them all rotates as well, circling around a lemon-yellow teapot in the center. If that's not enough to make you wibbly-wobbly, you can spin the wheel in the center of your teacup to start it spinning as well—as fast or as slow as you want! If you find yourself needing to sit down for a bit to recover after the ride, grab a cold drink from Blue Ribbon Cones next door—remember ice water is free—and find a nearby bench under a tree.

▶ Park Pointers

The first and most well-known version of a teacup ride is the Mad Tea Party, which opened in Disneyland in 1955. In the decades since, many ride manufacturers have designed and built similar rides. Dollywood's version opened in 2005 as part of a massive renovation and expansion of Country Fair. Lemon Twist will close when lightning is detected within 5 miles of the park; during heavy rain, snow, wind, or ice; when the temperature dips to 32°F or below; or during extreme heat.

Ride Operators

Dollywood hosts and ride operators are some of the friendliest folks around, and it's not hard to see that they love ensuring that everyone has a great time. Strike up a conversation with one of them and see for yourself. Some of them may even have a fun story to share!

8. The Amazing Flying Elephants

WHAT: Family-friendly flying elephant ride with lap belt restraints. No minimum height requirement, though riders under 48 inches tall must be accompanied by someone age 14 or older.

WHERE: Between Sky Rider and across from Lemon Twist. Part of an entire corner of rides that go round and round!

EXPERT TIP: For younger first-timers, keep the elephant on the ground to ease them into the ride. The next time, they may be ready to fly high!

▶ Why You Should See It

A classic ride that's appropriate for everyone in your group! The Amazing Flying Elephants takes you on a magical ride atop the backs of friendly flying elephants dressed in colorful capes. It doesn't matter which elephant you choose to ride since the experience will be the same regardless, so pick your favorite color, climb inside, and fasten the seat belt. As the elephants begin to rotate around the red star–emblazoned circus ball in the center, you have a choice about how to proceed. Keep rotating near the ground for the mildest experience or push the button to send your elephant up into the air! You're welcome to stay up high for the duration of the ride—the elephants will lower automatically at the end—or you can get crazy with the button and go up and down, up and down, as many times as you want. The flight lasts two-and-a-half minutes before crawling to a stop once the elephants have returned to ground level. When the kids have graduated from the miniature version of this ride—Busy Bees over in Happy Valley Farmyard—they'll be ready to take to the big(ger) skies on The Amazing Flying Elephants. Whatever your age, though, this is a classic ride that's a good time for all.

▶ *Park Pointers*

For younger riders who may be a little nervous, give them full control over whether or not the button that regulates the height of the elephant is pushed. Having some element of control will help calm their nerves until they realize this ride is not meant to be scary—just fun! When the temperature takes a dive—down to 32°F or lower—The Amazing Flying Elephants will close. The ride will also shut down during high winds, heavy rain, snow, or ice, or when lightning is detected within 10 miles of the park. Wait times for the Elephants are typically less than twenty minutes and sometimes as little as five minutes, and they tend to peak in the early afternoon.

Beat the Crowds

Festivals, holidays, and school breaks are peak attendance times for Dollywood. For a quieter park experience, aim for a midweek visit when most schools are in session. Try a Wednesday or Thursday during late August through early September between the summer and fall festivals for less congestion and shorter lines.

9. Sky Rider

═══════ FAST FACTS ═══════

WHAT: Soar high above the ground in patriotic-themed gliders with a rudder you can control! Uses over-the-shoulder restraints. Must be at least 42 inches tall to ride, and riders under 48 inches tall must be accompanied by someone age 14 or older.

WHERE: Across from Blue Ribbon Cones ice cream stand in Country Fair. You can't miss the gliders circling high above your head.

EXPERT TIP: See if you can grab an overhead view of the Dollywood Express coal-fired train during your flight.

▶ Why You Should See It

Fulfill your dreams of flying the friendly skies with Country Fair's Sky Rider, an aviator-style ride featuring two-person gliders that rotate around a tall center post. Like the other attractions in the western branch of Country Fair, Sky Rider is painted red, white, and blue with golden accents. Take advantage of the free cubbies at the end of the line to store any loose items—you don't want them taking their own flight while you're in the air! Choose your glider (hint: they're all the same) and get comfy. Once the shoulder harness is in place, it's time to fly! The rotating structure starts moving slowly, and you feel yourself lift off the ground, climbing and climbing into the air until reaching a height of 70 feet. The rotations pick up speed as the gliders naturally push out from the center.

Grab hold of the control handle between you and your ride partner to turn the rudders on either side of the glider and cause it to twist along its vertical axis. If you're content to leave well enough alone, however, just let the control stay in its neutral position to prevent the glider from twisting. After about forty-five seconds at the very top, the gliders will gradually descend until coming to a complete stop back on the ground. Start to finish, Sky Rider lasts for two-and-a half minutes of breezy fun and moderate thrills.

▶ Park Pointers

Sky Rider opened for business in 2005 and remains one of the more impressive rides in this corner of the park. It will close when lightning strikes are within 10 miles of the park, during high winds, during heavy rain or other extreme precipitation, or when the temperature drops below 36°F. The average wait time for Sky Rider is eleven minutes (on par with the rest of the Country Fair rides). This ride has an outdoor queue—like most in Country Fair—so keep stocked on water and sunscreen!

Smart Planning

Country Fair has the biggest draw for kids and young families, and many of these folks will make a beeline for the area soon after entering the park. For a better chance of avoiding crowds, wait until later in the day to head this way, when the congestion earlier in the day has cleared out.

10. Shooting Star

═══ FAST FACTS ═══

WHAT: Mini drop tower perfect for kids but still fun for adults. Uses over-the-shoulder restraints. Riders must be at least 36 inches tall to ride, and those under 42 inches tall must be accompanied by someone age 14 or older.

WHERE: In between the big grassy picnic area and Midway Market snack stand.

EXPERT TIP: Reach for the sky and swing your legs to get the most out of the drop!

▶ Why You Should See It

Shooting Star is perfect for drop ride newbies who want to test their courage on a shorter tower that will offer mild thrills for both kids and adults while still being a super-fun ride. The attraction consists of a double-sided star-spangled red, white, and blue structure with a six-person carriage on each side. Once you're tucked inside and the harness is lowered over your chest to keep you safe, the carriage begins its slow ascent to the top of the tower. Once there, you are left lingering at the top for an unpredictable amount of time, building the tension before a smooth drop to (almost) the bottom of the 25-foot tower. The fun doesn't end there, though, because as soon as you've oriented yourself, the carriage bounces up and down along the bottom third of the ride's height before rising to the top and repeating the whole thing again and again. The final thrill comes from a rise to the very tippy top and then a drop *allll* the way down. If you're wearing flip-flops or loose shoes, you may want to remove them before climbing into your seat. Or use this lesser-known theme park hack: Sit on them. Ask a friend or family member on the ground to snap some photos as you plummet to your doom! Just kidding, you'll be fine; this ride is pure fun! You're likely to walk right by Shooting Star while cruising through the middle of Country Fair on your way in or out, so be sure to stop and check it out!

▶ *Park Pointers*

This junior-sized drop tower debuted in Country Fair in 2005. It was a much family-friendlier version of more intense tower-style rides at Dollywood such as the now-defunct Timber Tower and, later, Drop Line over in Timber Canyon. Because you'll be lifted up toward the sky during this ride, Shooting Star will close when lightning strikes are detected within 10 miles of the park and during conditions of high wind, heavy precipitation of any kind, or temperatures lower than 36°F.

CHAPTER FIVE

The Village & Owens Farm

A quaint corner of Dollywood featuring one of the oldest and long-lasting attractions, The Village is where you can climb aboard an antique coal-powered train and take a relaxing ride through the foothills. But that's not all: You can also experience a tasty, fresh flatbread pizza for lunch; ride an antique carousel; and see one of Dollywood's most nostalgic multisensory shows.

Named for her "mother's people," Owens Farm has many references in both name and theme to Dolly's life. This area is Dollywood's smallest, anchored by play areas for the young'uns and a hair-raising high-thrills ride modeled after a popular homegrown leisure activity from the old days.

THE VILLAGE

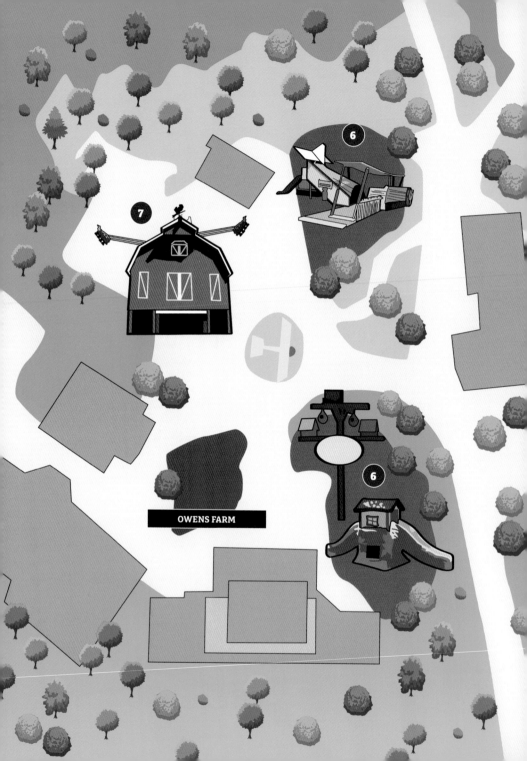

OWENS FARM

1. Village Carousel

WHAT: Beautiful hand-painted carousel with belt restraints. No minimum height requirement, though visitors under 42 inches must be accompanied by someone age 14 or older.

WHERE: On the border between The Village and Country Fair.

EXPERT TIP: Choose a favorite animal and race to claim it when it's your turn to ride!

▶ Why You Should See It

Dollywood's charming Village Carousel is the epitome of classic theme park rides. The ride is sheltered by a painted canopy with gingerbread trim and has an average wait time of less than ten minutes. There are sixty colorful animals to choose from, and your ride experience will be the same on any of them, so choose freely! The carousel doesn't feature only horses but also other four-legged creatures, such as zebras, antelopes, rabbits, and deer. There are even a few unexpected beasts like a pig, a giant rooster, and even an ostrich! Oh, and be on the lookout for a couple of fantastical dragons painted with shiny blue and green gradient scales. At the end of each cycle, the animals come to a stop anywhere from all the way lowered up to full height, so if you can't hoist yourself up to a taller seat, simply choose one that's come to rest closer to the ground. When the ride starts up, you're treated to the lively tinkle of traditional calliope music as the platform rotates at a brisk (but not *too* brisk) speed. The animals move up and down as you spin around, providing the illusion of a gallop. Village Carousel has been making riders smile since 1998, and it's pretty safe to say that it'll be sticking around as a favorite attraction for many years to come.

▶ Park Pointers

Riding with a very young toddler, baby, or someone with mobility issues that prevent sitting up on one of the creatures? Have a seat on one of the blue and gold benches on the carousel instead, and you'll still be able to enjoy the music and basic motion of the ride (no ups and downs) without needing to balance yourself. For the shortest lines, visit the carousel as soon as the park opens or just before it closes. The busiest time is the late afternoon. Village Carousel will close during extreme precipitation or when lightning is detected within 5 miles of the park.

Dolly the Horse

See if you can spot the painted horse with a mane of long and luscious blond hair—her name is Dolly!

2. Heartsong Theater

FAST FACTS

WHAT: Indoor theater featuring a heartwarming sensory journey through life in the Smoky Mountains as well as family-friendly live action performances.

WHERE: Quaint baby-blue building at the far end of The Village. The structure looks like a cross between an old country church and a colonial home.

EXPERT TIP: The shows are short and sweet, perfect for relaxing inside while waiting for the next boarding time for the Dollywood Express.

▶ Why You Should See It

Heartsong Theater brings the ambience of an outdoor theater to a comfortable indoor venue that features artificial trees and other greenery—giving the illusion of being seated among the flora of an enchanted forest. The theater's namesake show, *Heartsong*, is a twenty-minute film presentation about Dolly Parton's cherished Smoky Mountains. The mini feature, which debuted in 1994, was shot on 70 mm film by Jack Rouse Productions and features Dolly herself speaking and singing about her forever home amid beautiful footage of East Tennessee mountains and farmland. The show was the first to add special effects to enhance the feeling of immersion, including fragrances like flowers and apple pie, sprinkles of water during river and thunderstorm scenes, and leaves that float down from the ceiling. Though this is an older attraction, it's a nostalgic part of The Village's entertainment, and longtime Dollywood visitors enjoy it to this day. If you're a new Dollywood goer, give it a try if you have time and see if it gives you a heart full of warm and fuzzies after it's over. Also in the theater, The Imagination Playhouse features three upbeat twenty-minute sing-along shows: *Coat of Many Colors*, *The Little Engine That Could*, and *Violet the Pilot*. Check the schedule regularly to see which shows are on deck during your time in the park.

▶ Park Pointers

After Heartsong Theater opened during the 1994 season with its innovative *Heartsong* film, Dolly was overwhelmed by the response. Her intent was to create an attraction that would provide top-notch entertainment for guests, but she never expected the strong emotions elicited by the experience, highlighted by her original tune, "Heartsong." Because other attractions may close during more extreme weather conditions, the indoor theaters—any of them—are ideal places to wait out the elements, so grab a poncho or umbrella and head on over to take in a show!

 ### A Lifelong Passion

Despite her successes in film, business, and performing, Dolly has always considered herself a songwriter before anything else. During her expansive career, she has written about 3,000 songs! Her music spans the genres of country, gospel, pop, bluegrass, and even disco!

3. Dollywood Express

═══ FAST FACTS ═══

WHAT: A twenty-minute ride on Dollywood's real coal-fired steam engine with bench seating and no restraints. No minimum height or age requirement.

WHERE: Climb aboard at the train depot on the eastern side of The Village.

EXPERT TIP: The train runs hourly. Arrive at least twenty minutes before departure time to board the train.

▶ Why You Should See It

Experience one of Dollywood's oldest attractions, which opened in 1961, back when the park debuted as Rebel Railroad. Dollywood utilizes two authentic World War II 110-ton steam engines to power the Dollywood Express, taking guests on a relaxing ride through the park and foothills of the Smoky Mountains. The oldest of the two engines is nicknamed "Cinderella" and was built in 1938. It rotates in and out of operation with the second engine, nicknamed "Klondike Katie," which was built in 1943. During the war, both locomotives were used in Alaska to aid in the transportation of soldiers and supplies. Now, the engines are operational pieces of history that serve as an iconic feature of Dollywood, as there are not many places on the property where you can't hear the *chugga-chugga* of the wheels or the bellowing of the steam whistle. If you can get close enough to see the plaque on the side of the impressive engine, you can figure out which one will be powering your ride. Each train uses 2 tons of coal and 4,000 gallons of water daily to complete the continuous circuits around the perimeter of Dollywood.

The slow-moving ride is a gentle journey that departs The Village and moves through each section of the park while the tour guide explains the locations visible from either side of the train cars. You'll get glimpses of any new expansions under construction, plus the inside scoop on them, and at one point you'll cross right over Craftsman's Valley while being instructed to wave at the people (and Miss Lillian, if she's around) below. Make time in your day to experience the Dollywood Express and a piece of both American and Dollywood history.

▶ Park Pointers

Because this train is the real deal, tiny bits of soot are expelled from the smokestack on top of the engine. The soot is capable of staining light-colored fabrics or landing on your skin, in your hair, or even in your eyes. Keep this in mind before deciding to ride and consider wearing sunglasses for extra protection. The train cars are open-air, so sitting in the middle instead of on the ends may cut down on the amount of coal smoke you are exposed to. The train's whistle is quite loud, so if you're riding with younger folks or those sensitive to loud noises, consider sitting near the back of the train to add distance when the engineer lets it blow. The train will not operate when lightning is detected within 10 miles of the park, during high winds, or during extreme precipitation.

This Is a Robbery!

Up until 2003, the train ride included a staged robbery where disheveled bandits would appear from the woods and climb aboard the train with prop guns and pretend to hold up the train. Opinions were mixed about the performance, with some finding it too scary, and eventually it was removed from the tour.

4. Temple's Mercantile

WHAT: Multisection shop with apparel, train-themed merchandise, and toys.

WHERE: Directly across from the Dollywood Express depot. It looks like a country home attached to a wooden warehouse.

EXPERT TIP: This large climate-controlled shop is perfect for comfortable browsing during hot, cold, or rainy weather.

▶ Why You Should See It

Temple's Mercantile—also known as Temple's Warehouse—is the primary retail center of The Village. Located right across from the boarding area for the Dollywood Express, this is the place to go for a souvenir to remember your rail journey through the Smokies. The basics like coffee mugs, key chains, and apparel are here of course, and there's quite a selection of youth sizes! Toys are a major theme at Temple's, and you can also find mini trains, figurines, plushies, and all kinds of trinkets. The fun doesn't stop there, though, because there's also candy! Grab some sweet packaged snacks to keep in your bag for easy snacking later in the day, or get a small prepackaged meal (sandwiches or salads) from the coolers at the front of the store. When you're done collecting your loot, head outside and up the path a bit to check out themed live performances at the open-air Village

Depot Stage from such bluegrass and roots performers as Fiddling Leona with JP. Shows and shopping—an ideal Dollywood pairing!

▶ Park Pointers

The Temple family is a prominent name in Sevierville history. There was a Temple's Feed and Seed Store where weddings were conducted by County Commissioner Jimmie Temple. The name "Temple's Mercantile" is a tip of the hat to the family's place in Sevierville's community and economy. Temple's is a good place to pick up some essentials like sunscreen, basic medications, toiletries, baby supplies, umbrellas, and ponchos. With more than 2.5 million people visiting Dollywood each season, Dolly makes sure there is something for everyone. So even if you aren't big on rides, you can get your shop on in just about every section of the park.

Ch-Ch-Ch-Changes

When Dollywood opened in 1986, this area of the park was known as Village Square. Where Temple's Mercantile now stands used to be a general store back in those early days.

5. Iron Horse Pizza

WHAT: Casual eatery specializing in flatbread pizzas with choice of a rotating variety of toppings, as well as salads and kids meals.

WHERE: Next to the main shopping center in The Village, across the path that leads down the hill to Country Fair.

EXPERT TIP: For those of you who find yourself ordering "meat lover's" pizzas when calling up your favorite local delivery joint, go for the Klondike Katie!

▶ Why You Should See It

As one of Dollywood's two pizza-centric restaurants, Iron Horse Pizza has a straight-on view of Dollywood's coal-fired steam engine train and is an excellent place to sit and watch it come and go. The service inside is cafeteria-style; just grab what you want as you go through the line and then pay for it at the end. Staple menu options include the Klondike Katie pizza that is loaded with pepperoni, sausage, and bacon. For those who like to keep things simple, personal-sized pepperoni and cheese pizzas are also available. Daily specials may include a changing selection of pizzas and strombolis like Hawaiian, Italian white, Buffalo chicken, and barbecue chicken. Iron Horse tends to have limited-edition menu items that rotate in and out depending on availability. Yummy dishes found in the past have included harvest flatbreads with maple-flavored diced sweet potato and mascarpone and pesto flatbreads. Vegan pizzas (with meatless pepperoni and nondairy cheese) are also offered.

If you're not in the mood for something topped with sauce and cheese, you have a choice of garden salads and breadsticks, as well as packaged peanut butter and jelly sandwich meals for the kiddos to round out the menu. Iron Horse has lots and lots of outdoor seating, which is perfect even if you're not stopping here to eat and instead just need a shady spot to sit for a few minutes.

▶ Park Pointers

Prior to 2022, this location was known as Victoria's Pizza. The newly remodeled restaurant with a name that references the Dollywood Express (train... Iron Horse...get it?) opened with a revamped menu and additional outdoor seating in both an open-air deck and a shady covered pavilion with ceiling fans and lights. What sets Iron Horse apart from Lumber Jack's, Dollywood's other pizza restaurant, is that Iron Horse focuses on flatbread-style pizzas, while Lumber Jack's pizzas have a more traditional crust. Oh, and any pizza on Iron Horse's menu can be made with a gluten-free crust—just ask if you don't see it available in the self-service line.

6. Granny's Garden & Lil' Pilots Playground

―――――― FAST FACTS ――――――

WHAT: Themed playground areas for younger guests. Recommended for guests with a height of fewer than 48 inches. Those under 12 years of age must be accompanied by someone age 14 or older.

WHERE: On both sides of the main path leading into Owens Farm.

EXPERT TIP: No food is sold in Owens Farm, so pick up a snack and a drink before you head to the play areas to tide you over!

▶ Why You Should See It

When you arrive in the cozy mini area of Owens Farm, you'll find two quiet play areas where kids can burn off extra energy while the grown-ups take turns on the hair-raising Barnstormer or have a rest on a nearby bench. Turning left off the path will lead you to the corner housing Granny's Garden. This charming playground is geared to toddlers and younger kiddos and has a whimsical theme featuring friendly critters and colorful mushrooms. The structures are made with smooth materials, so there is no concern for splinters or sharp corners while your little ones play. If the weather's nice, there's a small water play area just across from Granny's

Garden with a coordinating nature theme, where kids can cool off on a hot day thanks to gentle fountains and water jets.

Hanging a right off the path will lead you to Lil' Pilots Playground. The main structure here is a large mock-up of a crashed biplane that is split between the nose and the tail with a small shady walkway under the upper wing. Kids can climb inside the nose and pretend to pilot the craft or climb up inside the tail and zoom down the slide out the back.

▶ Park Pointers

The play areas will close when there is lightning within 5 miles of the park or during times of extreme precipitation. Owens Farm is located right behind the historic Grist Mill in Craftsman's Valley, where Dollywood's famous and irresistible cinnamon bread is made. There is a back door to the Grist Mill from Owens Farm that *sometimes* offers a shortcut for those wishing to visit, though rumor has it that the door has been locked for good (can't hurt to check anyway). There's also a "secret" deck behind the Grist Mill with several picnic tables that few people know about, so they're almost always empty! The area where these playgrounds are located was formerly known as Daydream Ridge from 1987–2000, then as Dreamland Forest until 2011. Daydream Ridge had a toy shop and candy shop, a large playground, a glass shop, and a restaurant called the Daydream Diner. Dreamland Forest featured the world's largest interactive tree house, a water play area called Bullfrog Creek, a gift shop that sold nature-themed merchandise, and a restaurant called Ranger's Cookhouse.

 Dolly the Pilot...or Not

For the opening of Owens Farm, Dolly Parton showed up dressed as a fashionable World War I–era pilot. In reality, Dolly dislikes flying, rides, or being anywhere except on solid ground. She also has a fear of being on ships in large bodies of water and of being deep underground!

7. Barnstormer

FAST FACTS

WHAT: Exciting swinging pendulum ride with lap bar restraints. Minimum height requirement of 48 inches.

WHERE: Straight ahead when you enter Owens Farm—it's the only ride there, so you can't miss it!

EXPERT TIP: You'll rarely spend more than fifteen minutes waiting, but the shortest lines are in the evening during the hour before the park closes.

▶ Why You Should See It

Barnstormer is the primary attraction in Owens Farm, and it can certainly hold its own! The theme of this high-thrills ride is based on post–World War I stunt pilots, known as barnstormers, who purchased retired aircrafts to take thrill seekers on joy rides over local farmland. One such local who remembers these antics was Dolly's grandfather, Jake Owens, a music-loving preacher who gifted Dolly her first guitar when she was a little girl! The ride consists of two "airplanes," which are double-sided pendulums holding sixteen passengers each. Large banners on the fencing surrounding the ride introduce you to your fictional pilots: Rooster and Angel Flanagan, the "Dueling Daredevils." The vehicles are identical, so it doesn't matter where you sit or which direction you face—you'll get your hair blown backward (and forward) regardless as you zoom along at speeds as high as 45 mph.

Once you pass by a blue and gold biplane replica and through the supports of an old-fashioned windmill, you'll climb into your seat and be fastened tight. The pendulums start swinging, low and slow at first, then they pick up speed, completing stomach-tumbling 230-degree arcs with each cycle. When you reach the highest peak, you'll be an incredible 81 feet from the ground! The whole thing only lasts about a minute, but it's a minute you won't soon forget! Dollywood's roller coasters get all the hype, but Barnstormer is an underdog of an adrenaline rush that you'll want to ride again.

▶ *Park Pointers*

Owens Farm, Dollywood's smallest section, is tucked into a corner behind Craftsman's Valley. The area was named for both Dolly's mother's side of the family and the vice president of marketing and public relations at Dollywood, Pete Owens. The area opened as Owens Farm on March 26, 2011 and Barnstormer has been serving up screams and squeals to guests ever since. Because of the intense nature of this experience, it may be unsuitable for some guests even if they meet the height requirement. The ride will close due to several inclement weather conditions including high winds, temperatures below 32°F, heavy precipitation, or lightning within 10 miles of the park. Barnstormer, as well as several other Dollywood rides, has a test seat in front of the queue so that you can try out the restraint system if anyone in your group has concerns about fitting comfortably on the ride.

Mountain Slidewinder

Barnstormer wasn't always the only ride in Owens Farm: There used to be a high-speed toboggan-style water ride that wound down the hillside and that was in operation for thirty-one years, called Mountain Slidewinder. Reasons for its closure and later demolition were the increased cost of maintenance and the length of the path to get to the queue—it was quite a hike!

CHAPTER SIX

Craftsman's Valley

Appreciate the talents of Dollywood artisans demonstrating the creation of a variety of handicrafts along the shady hillside of Craftsman's Valley. Themed for the late 1800s, the area exemplifies traditional craftsmanship through quaint shops showcasing handmade goods, enticing home-cooked food, and top-notch entertainment. The sound of hammering, the scent of freshly hewn wood, and the glow of hot steel bring this area to life as talented craftspeople spend their days producing art using their hands and creativity. Witness beautiful items being created before your eyes, or, in some cases, participate in creating a custom souvenir to take back home with you. Get ready to step back in time and immerse yourself in the atmosphere of Craftsman's Valley, where every visit promises to be a journey into the heart of turn-of-the-century Appalachia.

CRAFTSMAN'S VALLEY

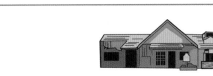

1. Miss Lillian's Mill House & BBQ Corner

WHAT: Cafeteria-style indoor restaurant with neighboring walk-up lunch stand cooking up tasty barbecue favorites, sides, and desserts.

WHERE: Across the path from the Grist Mill in Craftsman's Valley.

EXPERT TIP: At the Mill House, try the pulled pork–loaded baked potato for a great value hearty meal. At the Corner, go for an expertly smoked turkey leg that you can chew on while continuing on your way!

▶ Why You Should See It

The plumes of smoke billowing from the building that houses both Miss Lillian's Mill House and Miss Lillian's BBQ Corner are an obvious clue to what can be found inside. Whether you're looking to sit a while and enjoy a meal or pick up something to munch on while on the way to the next attraction, Miss Lillian will take care of you.

For a plate loaded with hot homemade vittles, Lillian's Platters are a menu highlight at Miss Lillian's Mill House. They come with a choice of entrée—hand-breaded Southern fried chicken, slow-smoked pork shoulder, smoked sausage, or smoked barbecue spice-rubbed ribs—and hot homemade corn bread. A choice of two mouthwatering side dishes like creamy mac and cheese, baked beans scented with maple, or Southern green beans completes the meal. Oversized baked potatoes are another enticing choice, and they can be loaded with chili, pulled pork, or even mac and cheese. If you want to keep things green, a variety of salads are on offer that are full of fresh vegetables and proteins like ham, turkey, or grilled chicken breast. If you save room for dessert, indulge in Miss Lillian's butter cake or strawberry cheesecake for a sweet finish.

For those looking for a quick grab-and-go meal, Miss Lillian's BBQ Corner is an open-air stand at the end of the restaurant building, and the strong aroma of smoked meats coming from within will get your tummy growling before you even realize you are hungry. Like at the Mill House, the items available at BBQ Corner change frequently, but some options you may find include succulent oversized turkey legs, smoked corn on the cob still in the husks, and juicy pulled pork sandwiches.

▶ Park Pointers

Prior to 2020, Miss Lillian's Mill House was an all-you-can-eat buffet, but safety considerations during and after the COVID-19 pandemic caused the establishment to undergo several changes, first shifting to family-style service followed by another update to a more traditional menu served cafeteria-style. Seating is available inside to enjoy the comforts of central heating or air-conditioning, depending on the time of year. Outdoor seating is available as well, both on the covered patio and farther out on the path. A group of tables is located behind Miss Lillian's BBQ Corner for those wanting to enjoy the fresh air away from the noisy flow of passersby. Proximity to the Grist Mill's waterwheel offers a serene view while dining. But don't be startled by the whistle of the Dollywood Express, which may pass right by on the nearby tracks. If the timing is right, you may even catch a glimpse of Miss Lillian herself!

2. Grist Mill & Cinnamon Bread

WHAT: Old-fashioned grist (aka grain) mill with working waterwheel serving up Dollywood's famous cinnamon bread.

WHERE: One of the most recognizable attractions in the whole park, located at the bottom of the Craftsman's Valley hill.

EXPERT TIP: Ask that your warm cinnamon bread be served with sweet buttercream or homemade apple butter!

▶ Why You Should See It

Craftsman Valley's beautiful Grist Mill attracts thousands of guests every season, all wanting to get their hands on the perfection that is Dollywood's bestselling treat: hot, ooey-gooey cinnamon bread. You know it's fresh because you can literally see it being made right behind the counter when you walk inside. Watch as Dollywood bakers dunk mounds of dough into melted butter before adding a generous coating of cinnamon and sugar. The dough is cut with deep grooves, which allow even more butter and cinnamon goodness to get inside the bread and yields an ideal "pull apart" shape once the dough is baked. On the other side of the kitchen, with a whoosh of the heavenly aroma of sweetened cinnamon and steaming yeasty bread, finished trays are taken from massive ovens. From the first bite, you're hooked. The outside is a sweet crust of crystallized sugar and cinnamon, the inside is tender yet slightly chewy, and the whole thing is deliciously buttery. It's best eaten when still warm, because you'll swear you hear harp music as soon as it passes your lips.

The park has reported that more than 200,000 loaves of cinnamon bread are sold each season, using close to 1,700 pounds of ground cinnamon. With numbers like that, it's clear that this treat is really something special, and no trip to Dollywood is complete without a taste. In addition to its signature delight, the Grist Mill also sells fresh fruit preserves, butters, and specialized syrups in flavors like strawberry rhubarb, blackberry, peach, and apple pie.

▶ *Park Pointers*

If you're passing the Mill and the line is *not* pouring out the door and down the hill, get in it! As the day lengthens, so does that line, so never pass up the opportunity when it's nice and short. The Grist Mill was constructed in 1982 and was the first fully functioning mill of its type built in Tennessee in over one hundred years. The waterwheel is a throwback to centuries gone by when Smoky Mountain folks used it to grind corn and wheat into cornmeal and flour. The mills were an integral part of community survival, since the milled grains could be preserved and used to keep everyone fed during the winter. Just inside the front entrance of Dollywood's Mill, look off to the left for a demonstration of how hydropower from the waterwheel outside is used to turn the large millstones.

Perk for Resort Guests

If you are a guest of Dollywood's DreamMore Resort and Spa, you can have cinnamon bread hand-delivered via room service to enjoy with a pot of hot coffee. Guests and nonguests alike can also purchase this sweet favorite at DM Pantry on the resort grounds.

3. Granny Ogle's Ham 'n' Beans

FAST FACTS

WHAT: Full-service indoor restaurant with a menu centered around the classic Southern combination of ham and pinto beans.

WHERE: Right next door to the open-air Valley Theater in Craftsman's Valley. The butter-yellow building has an inviting wraparound porch.

EXPERT TIP: Line up your arrival with showtimes for the theater next door and ask to be seated on the side that faces the stage so that you can enjoy your meal while listening to live music!

▶ Why You Should See It

As natural a pairing as peanut butter and jelly, ham and pinto beans just straight up belong together, and at Granny Ogle's Ham 'n' Beans, that's what they do best. The sit-down restaurant's signature meals include a hot pit ham dinner, ham and pinto beans with tender cooked greens, and a delicious pulled ham sandwich. Non-ham options are also available, including Dollywood's famous Meatloaf Stacker, a thick slice of toasted butter crust bread piled high with a slab of homemade meatloaf, creamy mashed potatoes, and gravy. Granny Ogle's tasty chicken potpie and chicken cassoulet are delicious choices as well. Every meal comes with a warm skillet of fresh corn bread boasting a perfect, crunchy crust. And while the whole of Dolly-wood has no shortage of tempting treats, you can enjoy some dessert right here in the form of classic banana puddin', a decadent mile-high peanut butter explosion (basically a heavenly peanut butter chocolate cake), or, for those with food sensitivities, gluten-free vegan brownies. While not overwhelming, the portions are generous, so bring your appetite along when you dine at this homey restaurant. Sit outside and breathe fresh mountain air while digging into your dinner.

▶ Park Pointers

The building that houses Granny Ogle's Ham 'n' Beans has been around for decades, but back in the 1970s it had a different identity: Big John's Ham & Beans. Pickers and pluckers stood on the front porch to entertain patrons as they chowed down on food that wasn't all that different from what's on the menu today (though the prices were *very* different!). Once Dolly Parton arrived on the scene, the restaurant was renamed after a beloved family member of her forever best friend, Judy Ogle. Dolly remembers going over to the real Granny Ogle's house to enjoy her home-cooked beans and corn bread. So now, when you step into Granny Ogle's Ham 'n' Beans, you're stepping directly into one of Dolly's fondest memories.

 Try It

Granny Ogle's is where you can find one of Dollywood's best appetizers: pimento cheese with the park's own barbecue pork rinds. It may sound strange, but it's delicious! You'll never want to use plain ol' chips for dipping ever again.

4. Smoky Mountain Christmas Shop & Valley Wood Carvers

FAST FACTS

WHAT: Double-occupancy shop selling all things Christmas and handmade woodcrafts.

WHERE: Just past the intersection to Owens Farm in Craftsman's Valley, up the hill from the Grist Mill.

EXPERT TIP: The shop is located near public restroom facilities. Convenient time for a bathroom break after you shop!

▶ Why You Should See It

It doesn't take long into a visit to Craftsman's Valley to notice a theme of handmade and custom goods. Updated in 2023, Smoky Mountain Christmas Shop & Valley Wood Carvers is where you can outfit your home for the holidays (or any time) with unique items and decor, most of which are handcrafted. The walls of ornaments will catch your eye as soon as you walk in, the colorful balls and baubles the ideal way to commemorate a trip to Dollywood. You can find ornaments featuring iconic park attractions such as the Dollywood Express train, the historical Robert F. Thomas Chapel, and the Grist Mill. While there's no lack of classic country Christmas colors like deep red and pine green as well as traditional patterns like buffalo plaid, you can also find more modern colors like frosty blue or chic black and white. One of the most popular features of the original Christmas store was the ability to personalize an ornament with names and dates, and you can still do the same at the shop's new Craftsman's Valley home!

Veteran Dollywood-ers might be confused at first by the new signage and festive theme inside this shop as of the 2023 changes, but look closer and you'll see that the intricately carved wooden items from the original Valley Wood Carvers are still there. Now they are showcased throughout the shop among the holiday cheer.

▶ *Park Pointers*

Prior to 2023, Valley Wood Carvers was all alone in its location and the Christmas shop was in Rivertown Junction. Back then, there was a beloved shop employee named Mary Ann who was battling an illness. She always said the shop needed a mouse, and master wood-carver, Billy Orr, a friend of Mary Ann's, decided to make that idea a reality. After Mary Ann retired due to her illness, Billy carved a small wooden mouse and placed it in a preexisting hole in the counter that Mary Ann always said looked exactly like a mouse hole. He sent Mary Ann a photo of the mouse to let her know that everyone was thinking of her. She loved hearing stories of the children who discovered the mouse and thought it was real! Though the shop was remodeled extensively when it started selling Christmas merch in 2023, Mary Ann's legacy was preserved, and you can still see the little wooden mouse today. The new location of the mouse hole is on the left-hand side of the fireplace near the floor. You may have to move some of the shop's items to find it, but it's there!

Robert Lee Parton

Dolly's daddy was no stranger to working with his hands, just like the artisan wood-carvers at Dollywood. The supportive father and husband took construction jobs on top of his farming and sharecropping duties to help support the large family.

5. Pork Rinds

WHAT: The crispiest and freshest pork rinds you'll ever eat. A Dollywood treasure.

WHERE: About a third of the way into Craftsman's Valley. Look for the galvanized buckets holding bags of pork rinds.

EXPERT TIP: Ask for a free sample before deciding which flavor(s) you want to purchase!

▶ Why You Should See It

What exactly is a pork rind? This tasty Southern-born snack is a delightful combo of salt and crunch, though looking too completely into exactly what it is may seem less appetizing to some. To create pork rinds, raw pig skins are first boiled in water, then trimmed of most of the fat layer. Next, the skins are placed into an oven on low heat for several hours to dehydrate. Finally, the dried skins are deep-fried in oil, where they become perfectly puffy and crispy. The finished pork rinds are seasoned as soon as they come out of the fryer and sold immediately for optimal flavor and texture. Dollywood has perfected the process of frying up pork rinds, and the walk-up stand's offerings will ruin you for the ones found in the chip aisle of your local grocery store. Certainly not a stereotypical theme park snack, the basic pork rind has been transformed at Dollywood into an indulgence that frequent visitors consider something not to be missed. The pork rinds are so fresh, there are signs cautioning about the hot grease pops coming from the massive frying vats as new batches are created in real time. Some flavors you might find on the menu include classic plain pork rinds, barbecue, salt and vinegar, and a special spiced seasoning called Tennessee Hot.

▶ *Park Pointers*

Pork rinds can be purchased in bags or in a refillable souvenir bucket. Come back any time during the season for a top off with fresh pork rinds at a deep discount, or you can have your bucket refilled with buttered popcorn or Kettle Korn. So whenever you're done with your in-park snacking, make sure to take advantage of the cheaper refills and have a snack for the ride home! While you're at it, pick up a refillable mug (available at Pork Rinds and other food stands) to save even more on drink refills. An all-season refillable mug will get you free refills for the entire season, and a single-day refillable mug is good for free refills that day and deeply discounted refills on subsequent trips.

That's a Lotta Pig Skin!

Each season, Dollywood hosts fry up and sell over 48,000 pounds of pork rinds, roughly the weight of one adult humpback whale. How many *Sunday Night Football* parties do you think that would cater?

6. Valley Forge Blacksmith

============ FAST FACTS ============

WHAT: Blacksmith shop with a variety of hand-forged and custom-created items.

WHERE: Through the big open entrances in a large, rust-red barn-like building with a curved facade.

EXPERT TIP: Celebrating a special occasion during your visit? Plan to surprise your loved one with a custom knife or sand-cast sign!

▶ Why You Should See It

Go ahead and jostle the collection of handmade wind chimes hanging near the entrance to Dollywood's blacksmith shop—you won't be the only one who can't resist making them sound their tinkling tones. Turn around and you'll see a large wooden coal bunker (yes, you can touch the coal too!) next to the barricade that offers a view of the demonstration area. Fireplace tools, handmade garden art shaped like butterflies, wall art crafted from hand-forged steel are some of the items up for sale in the front section of the shop. A room off to the side has smaller artisan wares, including beautiful handmade knives with glinting, sharp blades. Knife-making is one of the featured skills demonstrated every day by Dollywood craftspeople, and you can join in on the process by signing up for the Forge-Your-Own Knife experience. Folks taking advantage of this fun premium activity will get to see what it's like to be a blacksmith apprentice by assisting in the process of creating a knife from common objects such as a railroad spike, a horseshoe, or a bolt. The blacksmith grasps the object using large tongs and places it inside a super-hot crucible to allow the metal to be shaped. The glowing hot object is placed on an anvil, and then your help is needed to hammer it flat to create the shape of the blade. The final step is to stand back and watch as the blacksmith polishes and sharpens the brand-new blade. Each custom knife comes with a sheath and certificate of authenticity, and Gold-level season passholders will also receive a free gift.

▶ Park Pointers

Reservations to create a custom knife cannot be made via telephone or online. Visit the blacksmith shop early in the day to make a reservation in person. Your reservation will include a time slot for when to return later in the day. Keep in mind that participants must be at least 7 years old. No sandals or open-toed shoes are allowed in the smithing area. Aprons and face shields will be provided and must be worn at all times. Because Dollywood does not allow weapons on the property, your custom knife will be held at the Package Pickup counter at Dollywood Emporium for retrieval just before exiting the park. Prices for the experience vary depending on the type of knife made. The smaller bolt knives are the least expensive with the shortest experience time, while the railroad spike knives are the most expensive with a longer experience time. In addition to knives, the shop also takes custom orders for sand-cast signs that are created by placing patterns of numbers and letters in a template, which are then pressed into a flask of fine green sand used as a channel for molten aluminum to flow through and create the finished product.

 ### Did You Know?

Dolly Parton's hometown of Pigeon Forge got its name from a local nineteenth-century iron forge named after the nearby Little Pigeon River.

7. Hillside General Store

WHAT: Variety shop that exemplifies the power of Craftsman's Valley to make you feel like you've traveled over one hundred years into the past.

WHERE: Standing out among the line of retail shops along the Valley; the two-story building with board-and-batten siding.

EXPERT TIP: Just like in the old days, you can send a postcard to loved ones back home from the post office inside this general store.

▶ Why You Should See It

Hillside General Store, with its second-story sittin' porch, blue bay windows, and vintage signage, is like an entire department store squished into a single room (the upper floor of the building isn't accessible to visitors). Dollywood tried to re-create what a real general store would look like right down to mismatched wood display cabinets and old crates for showing off wares. You can purchase supplies for washin' up, like natural soap, bodywash, shave cream, and scented lotion. And like any well-stocked general store, kitchen items such as pitchers, bakeware, whisks, and other implements spill out of the tall shelving units. Because the weekly grocery shopping would have been done in shops like this back in the day, in Dollywood's version you can buy fruit preserves, honey, jarred vegetables, and single-serving snacks. There is also "by the pound" old-fashioned candy, and you can scoop as little or as much as you want. All your favorites from days gone by fill the wooden barrels, like Bit-O-Honeys, crispy Peanut Butter Bars, hard butterscotch, chewy vanilla caramels, and more. In the back corner, you'll find barrels and bins of vintage-style toys like hobbyhorses, jack-in-the-boxes, cap guns, jacks, and some more modern-day playthings as well.

▶ Park Pointers

General stores were an important part of American society in the 1800s and even into the twentieth century. They were set up so that patrons could sample the merchandise—either through touch, sight, or taste—before deciding to make a purchase. The stores usually carried basic food ingredients, clothing, toiletries, and other sundries. The space was a social hot spot as much as it was a place to buy your cornmeal and coffee. Folks would sit around a central stove, making small talk or playing checkers (psst, you can play a game of oversized checkers on the front porch of Hillside General Store!). Proprietors of these stores were known for their caring and courteous natures, offering credit lines to new farmers until they had enough crops and livestock to sell. Glass jars of penny candy were a typical sight along the counter, poised for those last-minute impulse purchases. Hillside General Store fits right in with the energy and aesthetic in Craftsman's Valley—it just wouldn't be the same without it!

8. Old Flames Candles

━━━━━━ **FAST FACTS** ━━━━━━

WHAT: Aromatic old-fashioned candle shop selling tapers, wax melts, and hand-carved candles.

WHERE: On the corner where the Craftsman's Valley path forks off up the hill to Daredevil Falls.

EXPERT TIP: If you're visiting on a hot day, go to the candle shop at the end of your stay so that your purchased candles don't get melty and marred by the Southern heat.

▶ Why You Should See It

"Old Flames Can't Hold a Candle to You" is a song Dolly Parton recorded in 1980 at the suggestion of her husband, Carl Dean. Dollywood's candle-making shop is named after the hit tune and takes a more literal definition of the title as it is full of all things wax and wicks! Prepare your olfactory system, because it's in for a treat the moment you step across the comfy covered porch that surrounds the warm and cozy shop. The glorious array of candles in any shape, color, and scent you can imagine fill every nook and cranny, punctuated by the shop's most coveted item: cut-and-carve candles. These beautiful candles are created by first taking a white paraffin base shape—usually a tapered star—and dipping it multiple times in several different colors of melted wax. Once the colors have been added, a final thick layer of color is added to conceal the rainbow inside. Then it's time for the cool part! The still-warm candle is hung from its wick, and the carver uses special tools to cut away small sections of wax and reveal the layers of dipped color. The sections are then twisted, curled, and reattached to the base, resulting in an exquisite decorative piece. The carvers must work quickly, since they only have about fifteen minutes before the wax hardens too much to be carved and shaped effectively. Once the design is complete, a small well is carved around the wick to allow the candle to burn cleanly down the center while preserving the cut and carved layers as much as possible. The finished candle gets a dip in a clear glaze for a glossy shine, and then it's left to dry for about three hours before it can be sold.

Beyond the hand-carved candles, the shop sells an exclusive line of wax melts and votives in lovely fragrances (psst...look for the cinnamon bread scent!). And if you haven't had lunch yet, your appetite may be triggered by the sweet-smelling—and realistic-looking—wax ice cream sundaes. Even more, there are shelves stocked with handmade bath and body products to bring home if you want to relax in a tub of steaming bathwater while burning your new candles.

▶ Park Pointers

Feeling inspired by watching the candle-carving process by Dollywood artists? Get into the action by dipping your own candle to take home with you. Choose from an impressive variety of candle sizes and shapes, including mushrooms, hearts, stars, trains, Christmas trees, snowmen, pumpkins, and so much more. A park host will give you the rundown on how to dip your candle, and you'll have your pick of colors from the vats of melted wax—over a dozen different hues—to create your perfect result. Coat your creation in a single color or layer it for a gradient effect. Either way, you'll end up with something totally unique to take home with you. The only problem is that the candles are so pretty, you may have trouble with wanting to burn them!

9. Robert F. Thomas Chapel

FAST FACTS

WHAT: Single-room wooden church conducting worship services each week.

WHERE: Up the path from the bald eagle enclosure next to a tree-covered hillside.

EXPERT TIP: Visiting the park close to Christmas? Enjoy the melodic voices of gospel carolers on the chapel's front steps.

▶ Why You Should See It

Built in the style of Appalachian architecture at the dawn of the twentieth century, the Robert F. Thomas Chapel was erected in 1973 when the park was still known as Goldrush Junction. That same year, Dolly included a song about the chapel's namesake on her autobiographical album, *My Tennessee Mountain Home.* At the time, the park was closed on Sundays, as were most other businesses in the area. With the introduction of weekly church services, Goldrush Junction started to have Sunday hours for believers who wanted to worship on park grounds. The chapel was named for a doctor and preacher in Sevier County who was staunchly loyal to the community and had a personal mission to ensure that more people had access to good healthcare. As he was known for making house calls, Dr. Thomas ended up delivering Dolly Parton in her home on January 19, 1946, nearly three decades before the chapel would be named for him and just shy of forty years before the park was renamed Dollywood. Today, a painting of Robert F. Thomas arriving to deliver baby Dolly hangs on a wall in the chapel.

The chapel is full of history thanks to many generous donations from local community members. The bell hanging in the chapel steeple rings before each service, and to this day, guests of Dollywood can have the honor of making the bell sing. The bell was a donation from the Williamsburg School, facilitated by Mrs. Brad King, and was dedicated to her father, a man named John Emert. The doors leading into the one-room chapel were made by trustees of Pleasant Hill United Methodist Church in 1981 and later donated, and some of the old wooden pews came from the same church. The restored wooden piano is over 120 years old, making it fit right in with the late-nineteenth-century theme. The instrument was donated by former Dollywood employee Michael Stinnett. And that's not all! The chapel's windows came from Sevier County's first secondary school, Nancy Academy, built in the 1800s, and a carved likeness of Jesus Christ holding a lamb was donated by Dollywood's own woodcrafters. Behind the statue, a hexagonal piece of stained glass from the turn of the twentieth century hangs as a colorful tribute to Goldrush Junction personality "Deacon" Davis, who is credited with bringing worship services to an amusement park.

▶ Park Pointers

Religious services are held in the chapel at 11:30 a.m. every Sunday during non-festival days throughout the Dollywood season, and at 3 p.m. during Dollywood's Smoky Mountain Christmas. The holiday festival is also an ideal time to see the chapel strung with endless white lights. While visiting, guests can write their prayer needs on a list—anonymously, if preferred—and at the end of the year, all the requests are bound in a massive leather-covered volume by Dollywood's chaplain, Joey Buck.

What a Deal!

The Parton family gave Dr. Thomas a bag of cornmeal as payment for assisting in the birth of Dolly Parton.

10. Daredevil Falls

WHAT: Log flume–style ride with a thrilling drop and a big splash. Riders must be a minimum of 42 inches tall.

WHERE: The entrance is located about halfway through Craftsman's Valley. The ride will take you up, up, up the hill!

EXPERT TIP: Though they're moving slowly, the boats don't stop for people both entering and exiting the ride. Something to keep in mind for those with balance or mobility issues.

▶ Why You Should See It

While those really looking to get wet should head over to Dollywood's Splash Country, Daredevil Falls will get the job done just fine. When it's your turn to board, you'll step into an empty (and already wet) hollowed-out log serving as a boat, two folks per row, as it moves slowly through the water. Each boat has a name painted onto the bow, like *Sawtooth Tom*, *Sugarland Slider*, and *Crawdad Crawler*. The boat then moves swiftly down the rushing waterway, occasionally bumping against the sides as it travels through some lovely scenic Smoky Mountain nature. You'll pass through a cool, dark cave full of glowing, blinking bat eyes (don't worry, they aren't real!) and then continue down the waterway as you get sprinkled with sprays of water and small splashes. After passing through an abandoned logging camp, you'll begin the agonizingly slow climb to the top of the hill, only to splash down a tiny teaser drop before passing through a structure with a giant saw buzzing away. After a curve to the left, you see it: the 60-foot-steep drop that'll send your boat careening downward at a wild 50 mph before creating a monstrous splash at the bottom, soaking everyone in the boat—and spritzing onlookers.

▶ *Park Pointers*

Log flume and similar rides derived from troughs used to transport logs from the tops of hills or mountains down to sawmills using the natural downhill flow of water. Sometimes, loggers would ride the logs down the flumes to make sure things were operating as expected, and this later became a recreational activity known as "shooting the flume." Dollywood's version of a log flume ride uses a larger boat and slightly wider "flume" than is typical and is one of the fastest in the country. Dollywood used to have a true log flume ride called Country Fair Falls that was removed in 2004, making way for kid-friendly rides in that section of the park. Daredevil Falls opened on April 18, 1998, so there was some overlap in the operational seasons of the two rides. Daredevil Falls will close during high winds and extreme temperatures, when lightning is detected within 10 miles of the park, and during heavy precipitation.

 ### Dolly's Brothers Were Daredevils!

Daredevil Falls is named for Dolly's brothers, whose daredevil behavior visiting a dangerous water hole to play and swim she remembers. The swimming hole was kept full by a nearby waterfall, and sometimes her brothers would ride right over the falls into the waters below.

11. Eagle Mountain Sanctuary

═══ FAST FACTS ═══

WHAT: Bald eagle sanctuary and educational demonstration of Dollywood birds of prey by the American Eagle Foundation (AEF).

WHERE: Along the wooded hillside in Craftsman's Valley. Look for picnic tables and listen for the melodic calls of the eagles!

EXPERT TIP: Grab a delicious lunch from Hickory House BBQ to enjoy while watching the eagles and before seeing the *Wings of America* show. There's a lot of reasons to hang out a while in this section of the park.

▶ Why You Should See It

The steep hillside along the paths of Craftsman's Valley is home to the largest aviary for non-releasable American bald eagles in the US. All the eagles in the sanctuary receive loving care and an enriching environment from members of the American Eagle Foundation. The 30,000-square-foot (400,000 cubic foot!) aviary is separated into different enclosures for nesting pairs and bachelor and bachelorette eagles and a ground-level space for birds with limited or no flight capability due to injury or disability. For their safety, these birds are kept in a smaller, separate area, where you can get even closer to one of America's most treasured avians.

In between the eagle sanctuary and viewing area for other birds of prey, you'll find the Wings of America Theater, where you can be amazed by a dramatic show-and-tell featuring the amazing birds that call Dolly-wood home. One by one, handlers bring out birds and give audience members an intimate view of each one while wandering up and down the aisles offering interesting information about their habitat, diet, hunting or scavenging behavior, and conservation needs and efforts. Each show is a little different depending on the availability and health of the animals, but birds featured include falcons, vultures, hawks, owls, and of course, a magnificent bald eagle. Large screens flank each side of the stage with illustrative photos and video footage of the featured bird. Due in part to the efforts of Dollywood and AEF's partnership, bald eagles were removed from the endangered species list on June 28, 2007. You can contribute to the efforts to save endangered species of birds by offering donations at the end of the show...in a super fun way! Those who want to donate will line up near the stage while Friar Tuck, an African pied crow, stands over the cashbox and takes the donations right out of their hands (don't worry, he's nice!) before stuffing the cash into the slot.

▶ *Park Pointers*

The American Eagle Foundation (AEF) has been a part of Dollywood since 1990, and Dolly herself was present to release the first eagle into the sanctuary in 1991. Members of the AEF put on four showings of *Wings of America* each day throughout the regular season. During the twenty-minute show, the birds are trained to swoop down very close to the heads of audience members as they fly from one end of the theater to the other, so those who are squeamish about birds should keep that in mind.

Eagle When She Flies

Dolly has said she feels a connection with eagles since they are strong birds who fly fast and high. She references the magnificent birds in several of her songs and has said that when she's not writing about angels, she's writing about eagles and butterflies!

12. Hickory House BBQ

WHAT: The best place in the park to go for Dollywood's award-winning smoked barbecue.

WHERE: Located in the most peaceful area of Craftsman's Valley across from the enclosures of the Eagle Mountain Sanctuary.

EXPERT TIP: Getting full? Bring a friend and split meals so that you have room to try more delicious vittles during your visit.

▶ Why You Should See It

Get ready for the best lunch spot in the park! *Amusement Business* named Hickory House's smoked barbecue pork sandwich the best pork barbecue of any theme park in the US, and is it ever tasty! The Hickory House team prepares its meat fresh every single day, the pork and beef spending long hours in the smoker—fourteen hours for the pork and six-and-a-half hours for the brisket—until it falls apart and practically melts in your mouth. The meat is seasoned with a special (and top secret) blend of spices, pulled or sliced by hand, and stacked onto warm buns. Drizzle the meat with bold Memphis-style barbecue sauce, and you've got one hearty sandwich. Favorite menu items include a pulled pork smoked barbecue or sliced smoked brisket sandwich served on a warm brioche-style bun. A generous helping of cheesy and saucy pulled pork served over a bed of fries and topped with chopped scallions is another choice that won't steer you wrong. Giant smoked tom turkey legs, beautifully golden and boldly seasoned, are another tasty choice. Got a voracious appetite? Go for The Big Bear Feast, which is a belly-busting meal consisting of a sandwich loaded with both sliced smoked brisket and pulled pork smoked barbecue bathed in white Cheddar and barbecue sauces. All sandwich meals are served with a side of sidewinder fries, which are kind of a cross between a steak fry and a curly fry. Potatoes are cut thick into a fun curvy shape and then seasoned and deep-fried until perfectly crisp. If smoked meats really aren't your thing, you can get fried chicken tenders or a chicken Caesar salad as your main dish.

▶ *Park Pointers*

Hickory House BBQ draws quite a crowd wanting to sample Dollywood's blue-ribbon smoked barbecue pork, and thankfully ample seating is available around the establishment. You're gonna need it, because the juicy and sauced-up barbecue meals are as messy as they are delicious. Just adjacent to the building is a large pavilion with rows and rows of picnic tables. The structure catches a nice breeze during the hot seasons, and outdoor heaters are added during the cold months. There are also other picnic tables scattered around—with and without umbrellas—and across the path is a seating area between the hillside enclosures of the bald eagle sanctuary and the ground-level habitat for the eagles with no flight ability. Sounds like a good place for a midday picnic, eh?

Gettin' By

When Dolly first went to Nashville to further her music career, she filled salt and pepper shakers and ketchup and mustard bottles at a local place called Couser's Southern Restaurant in exchange for free food. She loved their barbecue in particular!

13. Lucky 7 Mine & Pick-A-Pearl

WHAT: Shop for stones and minerals, mine for gems, or discover your own beautiful pearl inside a real oyster.

WHERE: Across from the Wings of America Theater. You'll see the wooden gem-mining troughs under the shop's shed roof.

EXPERT TIP: If you purchase one of the larger mining bags, don't pour all the sediment out at once. Work with small amounts at a time so you don't miss out on tiny gemstones that might be hiding in there.

▶ Why You Should See It

Lucky 7 Mine & Pick-A-Pearl is a fun little stop in Craftman's Valley that will appeal to those who love to shop, as well as those who love to get their hands a little dirty. Have a go at being a real-life treasure hunter with Dollywood's own mining sluice! On the back wall of the shop, you'll find shelves stuffed with mining rough—sediment with gems hidden inside—sold in bags of varying sizes. This is where you'll start. The smallest bags are the most inexpensive but will yield fewer sparklies than the larger ones. Choose a bag to purchase, grab a spot at the mining sluice, and select a tray. Pour the sediment into the tray, lower it into the flow of water, and shake it back and forth gently to separate the riches from the dirt and silt. Once you've collected your treasures, you can identify your gems using a card given to you by staff that describes the gems and minerals you may find. Friendly Dollywood hosts are also available to give you some fun history about the stones.

Against the back wall of the store is the Pick-A-Pearl tank, Lucky 7's other unique souvenir station. The way it works is simple: Choose an oyster from the tank and ask a Dollywood host for help. Watch as the preserved oyster is opened (be prepared, they can be a bit stinky!), revealing your very own pearl. The size and color of the pearl you get is a total surprise! Next, browse the selection of pearl cages—specialized jewelry designed to hold loose pearls—to keep your pearl safe and secure.

One you've scored your special souvenirs, you can check out the rest of the store, which is full of everything that sparkles and shines. You can find loose gems and minerals that have been cut and polished, as well as other gifts like jewelry and gemstone-laden trees.

▶ Park Pointers

The pre-stocked bags at Lucky 7 Mine will guarantee that you take home a collection of pretty stones that originated from all over the world, but what about right there in Tennessee? While Dolly's home turf isn't the first place that comes to mind when you think of a gold rush or major mining operation, Tennessee has plenty of common minerals like quartz and pyrite (fool's gold) hidden in its hills. More rare finds include freshwater Tennessee river pearls, sapphires, and star-shaped marine fossils called crinoids.

Speaking of Pearls

When Dolly was just starting out in the music world, she had two mentors: country and western performers Pearl and Carl Butler. Pearl didn't have children of her own. She helped Dolly by buying her pretty things to wear onstage and encouraging her over-the-top look.

14. Calico Falls Schoolhouse

=== FAST FACTS ===

WHAT: Single-room mock-up of what a typical schoolhouse in East Tennessee would have looked like during the late-nineteenth and early-twentieth centuries.

WHERE: You'll find this cute little log cabin right next door to Blazing Fury. It has a red front door and dovetail corners and a school bell perched on top of the roof.

EXPERT TIP: Check out the Cram's map of Tennessee on the right-hand wall of the schoolhouse. George F. Cram was a prolific map publisher who fought in the Civil War.

▶ Why You Should See It

What turn-of-the-century town would be complete without a place for the young'uns to get an education? Calico Falls Schoolhouse is a charming re-creation of what a classroom setting was like around the year 1901. The inside of the schoolhouse is as bare-bones as it gets. While you're not able to actually go inside and walk around, you can stand at the open door opposite a wrought iron gate and peek inside. There's wide plank flooring, exposed rafters, and a small woodstove for warmth during the winter. A blackboard is centered on the front wall with a Bible verse intended for memorization. The desks in the classroom are the classic "fashion desk" style of the late 1800s, with a bench seat connected to the front of the desk.

When organized in rows, this bench seat design provides seating for the desk in front of it. The primary tool used in classrooms at the time—a writing slate—sits on each desk next to an inkwell and a sponge that is used for erasing marks made with shale or chalk. Lighting is provided via windows on either side of the room as well as by oil lamps mounted on each wall (pay no mind to the electric lights in the ceiling!). There's even a dunce cap on display, and yes, such a thing was actually used as a disciplinary tool for children who were disruptive or who fell behind in their studies. Students being punished with the cap were made to sit on a stool in a front corner of the classroom while wearing the humiliating headwear. Thankfully, this fell out of practice by the 1950s. Though the schoolhouse only takes a few minutes to stop by—maybe on your way into or out of Blazing Fury—it's a fun spot to enjoy!

▶ *Park Pointers*

As one of Dollywood's quiet and often overlooked attractions, Calico Falls Schoolhouse has been part of the park since it opened under the Dollywood name in 1986. While it may not be as interactive as some of the other park attractions, it's an important piece of both Dollywood and Smoky Mountain history. After you're done taking a peek inside, don't miss the list posted on the outside of the cabin setting forth some pretty absurd rules that teachers back in 1901 had to follow. A few examples are prohibitions against schoolmistresses keeping company with men, loitering downtown in ice cream parlors, and traveling outside of town limits without written permission.

Schoolgirl Dolly

Though Dolly's not old enough to have had a one-room schoolhouse experience, she attended a small school in Sevier County called Caton's Chapel (or just "The Chapel" to locals) in the 1950s. It was still common during that time for children to attend school in bare feet!

15. Blazing Fury

WHAT: A mild-thrills indoor roller coaster with lap bar restraints. Guests must be at least 42 inches tall to ride.

WHERE: Near the top of the hill of Craftsman's Valley. If walking downhill, you'll need to double back to see the entrance to the ride off to the side of the path.

EXPERT TIP: Look for references on the ride to retired Dollywood attractions—Flooded Mine and Timber Tower— as well as the road sign with all the former names of the park!

▶ Why You Should See It

Experience one of Dollywood's oldest and most nostalgic rides! While Blazing Fury is technically a roller coaster, you won't find any loops, high speeds, or daring drops while cruising along its tracks, making this a fun attraction for everyone. Ride along through the chaos of an 1880s town that has gone up in flames as the townsfolk scramble to escape and firefighters work to control the spreading blaze. With its old-school animatronics and handmade scenery, Blazing Fury is very much adored by Dollywood loyalists, and they wouldn't have it any other way.

Though the situation in the fictional town is dire, the dialogue is lighthearted. Molly, an animatronic damsel in distress attempting to leap from the balcony of a burning hotel into the net of a fireman with a weak back, is one of the more memorable characters. Quirky details abound in the displays, such as a menu board advertising specials like "scorched eggs" and "burnt toast." But don't worry, no actual fire rages: It's all flickering red lights and special effects that create the smoldering city. The most exciting part of the ride comes near the end with a series of quick drops as the train careens off a broken bridge and down a hill while a panicked voice yells, "Fire in the hole!" While longtime park veterans might consider it a necessity to carve out some space in their day for a ride on Blazing Fury, new visitors will be able to appreciate it as a piece of pre-Dollywood history.

▶ Park Pointers

Blazing Fury was built in 1978, a year after the park was named Silver Dollar City. Up until 1989, when Thunder Express was installed, Blazing Fury was the only roller coaster on the property. Some of the props and mannequins used in the town scenes were purchased from an old Gatlinburg haunted house, and others were crafted by hand. Be sure to ride during the holiday season to see the Christmas lights that bedazzle the doomed town! Because the ride is fully indoors, it is not affected by the elements and should remain open during inclement weather conditions.

Making a Splash

Prior to 2011, the "big" drop at the end of Blazing Fury (only about 22 feet) featured a splashdown into a pool of water. Because of damage to the ride vehicle and tracks from the moisture, it was ultimately removed.

16. Tennessee Tornado

═══════════ **FAST FACTS** ═══════════

WHAT: Twisting, looping, and spiraling roller coaster with over-the-shoulder restraints. Riders must be a minimum of 48 inches tall.

WHERE: Look for the vertical loop of the red track set back from the path at the top of Craftsman's Valley. You may even hear the screams and squeals of riders as the car rockets down the track.

EXPERT TIP: The front row is the place to be to feel the full intensity of the funnel!

▶ Why You Should See It

East Tennessee locals are no strangers to mighty thunderstorms during the warmer months, and Tennessee Tornado gives riders a taste of what it might be like to be whipped up inside a tornado that is slamming through the fictional Tennessee Mining Company. The experience feels like being inside a mine cart as the mighty spiral of wind has its way with you. The queue starts in a building that is already falling apart from previous storms, with loose boards and debris protruding from the walls. Once you're seated and buckled in tight, the cart leaves the station and you travel through a shed while hearing the distant wail of a tornado warning system. A climb up a chain lift hill precedes the first drop before you zoom around a curve and down a perilous 128-foot drop through a tunnel and then into the first inversion—a 110-foot-tall vertical loop. Before you have a chance to catch your breath, the cart turns and goes flying into a second vertical loop before immediately flipping you upside down again. After several more turns, the raging storm dissipates, and the cart slows to a stop back at the station. The whole experience only lasts one minute and forty-eight seconds, though you'll feel like you've been put through the ringer (in a fun way!) once your feet are back on solid ground!

▶ *Park Pointers*

Tennessee Tornado has been sending guests swirlin' and twirlin' since just before the turn of the century on April 17, 1999. The ride reused the same station as the now-defunct Dollywood coaster Thunder Express and cost a whopping $8 million to build. The track's signature element is nicknamed "Dolly's Iron Butterfly," which consists of a vertical loop and a sidewinder placed back-to-back. In combination, these parts of the ride trace the shape of a butterfly. The name of the maneuver comes from one of Dolly's own nicknames, given to her by her colleagues due to her sharp business sense. The coaster was designed by Arrow Dynamics and was one of their first computer-designed rides. The tracks and supports were engineered by Ride Centerline. Tennessee Tornado will close when the temperature outside reaches 34°F or below, when lightning is detected within 10 miles of the park, during high winds, and during heavy precipitation.

Keeping Calm in a Storm

When Dolly was a child, a tornado touched down in her holler, forcing her mama, Avie Lee, to think on her feet. Without scaring her eleven children, Avie Lee told everyone to turn the furniture upside down and place it against the wall, pretending it was a game. The family prayed and the house, miraculously, was unharmed by the storm.

CHAPTER SEVEN

Wilderness Pass & Timber Canyon

WILDERNESS PASS

TIMBER CANYON

Wilderness Pass is where the wild, untamed side of the Smokies is celebrated. Attractions vary from safe play areas for younger folks to one of the most thrilling roller coasters in the park, its bright blue track looming high up on the ridge overlooking the mingling crowds. Here you can grab a funnel cake, hot dog, and other snacks to keep you going while exploring this alluring section of Dollywood.

Timber Canyon is a chance to experience life in an Appalachian logging community in the late nineteenth century. Exciting rides like a high-speed wooden roller coaster and a massive drop tower are dispersed along the long and narrow pathways of the area. Wooded, shady surroundings and rustic architecture make for a bona fide look into the Smoky Mountains of yesteryear.

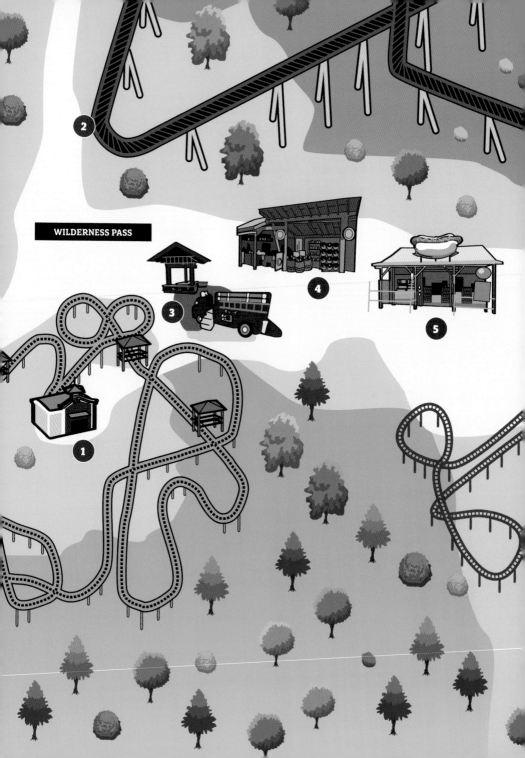

WILDERNESS PASS

TIMBER CANYON

1. FireChaser Express

WHAT: A family-friendly, dual-launch roller coaster with lap bar restraints. Riders must be at least 39 inches tall, and riders under 48 inches must be accompanied by someone age 16 or older.

WHERE: Tacked onto the hillside of Wilderness Pass amid thick greenery and a rushing waterfall.

EXPERT TIP: Sit in the front of the train for the biggest thrill during the backward launch. Sit toward the back for a better view of the pyrotechnics at the end of the ride.

▶ Why You Should See It

March 22, 2014, marked the opening of Dollywood's $15 million steel coaster, themed to represent the volunteer fire departments near the Great Smoky Mountains in the 1940s. FireChaser Express was built on the site of the former Adventure Mountain, a ropes and obstacle course that closed after only three seasons. FireChaser Express is fun for both grownups and kiddos—the ones meeting the height requirement, of course—and features drops, curves, camelbacks, and six moments of airtime! If you shy away from rides that go upside down, don't worry, because your fire truck (correction: fire *train*) remains upright during your adventure.

As the nation's first dual-launch roller coaster, FireChaser Express takes you on a fictional journey to assist fire chief Pete Embers with his attempts at dealing with local fireworks enthusiast "Crazy" Charlie Cherribaum. Charlie has a reputation for crying wolf, calling into Fire Station 7 several times a day concerned about a suspected fire danger (or just otherwise taking up the time of the volunteer firefighters). As the station's newest volunteer, you're tasked with answering an emergency call—this time a real one—to check out a rumor that Charlie has been creating a massive firecracker in secret. After being launched out of the fire station toward Charlie's Gas Station and Fireworks Emporium, you get glimpses of the results of Charlie's other failed fireworks experiments as you race along the track at a top speed of 35 mph before lurching to a halt inside Charlie's storage warehouse. Here, you confirm the presence of Big Bertha, Charlie's not-so-safe pyrotechnic creation. To escape the building before getting blown to smithereens, the coaster blasts out of the building backward and takes you on a swervy-curvy reverse ride before finally returning to the station.

▶ Park Pointers

The ride's theming is immersive and thrilling but shouldn't be too scary for younger riders. Smoke, sparks, and flames are seen as Big Bertha ignites, and loud bangs are heard. Depending on where you're seated, heat can be felt from the fire effects. If you miss out on some of the ride's details while zooming along the track, make sure to wander along the pathway near the queue for a view of the hillside and several great photo ops, including a bright red authentic 1941 fire truck! While waiting in line, direct your attention to the real fire hoses dangling from the ceiling just inside the main building of Fire Station 7. More than 1,300 hoses were donated and signed by brave firefighters across the state of Tennessee.

2. Wild Eagle

═══ FAST FACTS ═══

WHAT: Soar like an eagle on this unique wing-style roller coaster with shoulder harness restraints and a belt between the legs. Riders must be between 50 and 78 inches tall.

WHERE: The massive 12,000-pound bald eagle statue in Wilderness Pass, with 56-foot wingspan and intimidating chrome claws, will guide your way to the ride queue.

EXPERT TIP: If you dare, grab a seat in the front row and experience the spine-tingling pause at the top of the first drop as you dangle right over the edge of the hill.

▶ Why You Should See It

Experience one of the most unique roller coasters in the country! When you climb aboard Wild Eagle, you'll feel as though you've transformed into a majestic bald eagle soaring over the treetops of mountainous East Tennessee. It's easy to see what makes this first winged coaster in the US special just by looking at it. The coaster car seats riders on either side of the track—not above or below it—giving the appearance of actual wings. Each row has a larger-than-life figure of a bald eagle in the center of four seats, so you literally *are* the wings of the colossal avian. Your feet hang free once you're strapped into the car, and after you set out on the buttery-smooth ride along the modern steel track, the ride really does mimic the graceful mechanics of feathery flight. Just after you leave the station, a long, slow chain lift hill brings you to the highest point of the ride at 210 feet before sending you down the ride's biggest and most scream-inducing drop. From there, your flight takes you up through a large vertical loop, then almost immediately inverts you again in a tight roll. The long track spans 3,127 feet and has seemingly back-to-back thrilling elements that'll send you flying at a top speed of 61 mph and completing a total of four inversions. At the end of the two-minute, twenty-two-second ride, you'll come in for a landing after a sharp banked curve and nice and easy slowdown back into the station. Dolly hoped for the most unencumbered feeling of flight for riders of Wild Eagle, and this truly special attraction delivers on all points.

▶ Park Pointers

Wild Eagle opened to its first set of riders on March 24, 2012. (Although it was first announced the previous fall during Knoxville's massive Labor Day fireworks show, Boomsday, against a backdrop of a laser image of an animated bald eagle.) The Bolliger & Mabillard coaster was no cheap investment, costing the park $20 million to construct. On your way to ride this behemoth, you'll walk right past the stand housing SkyView Snacks, so if you have a longer wait ahead of you, it's a perfect opportunity to grab some popcorn or a butterfly pretzel. Oh, and don't forget to take a photo in front of the bald eagle statue and Dollywood sign whether you ride or not—it's a great souvenir! The queue for Wild Eagle is, for the most part, covered and shady, though keep in mind the ride will close during strong precipitation, lightning within 10 miles of the park, high winds, or temperatures that drop below 34°F.

 ### Golden Ticket Winner

In 2012, Wild Eagle won *Amusement Today*'s Golden Ticket Award for Best New Ride (Amusement Park), beating out five other nominees.

3. Firehouse Fun Yard

FAST FACTS

WHAT: Firefighter-themed playground and water play area recommended for younger children under 48 inches tall and supervised by someone age 14 or older.

WHERE: You'll find this cute little recreation area right up underneath the tracks of FireChaser Express.

EXPERT TIP: Bring swimwear or a set of dry clothes for warm days when the water jets are turned on!

▶ Why You Should See It

When visiting a theme park with young children, it's supremely helpful to know about all the kiddo-friendly areas for when they need a break for some free play. Firehouse Fun Yard is one such place that should be on your radar! Dollywood signage lists the structures here as "soft play," which means there are no sharp corners on which little noggins might bang or little knees bump. Shade sails hanging overhead, and nearby trees offer filtered shade when the sun is high. When the weather is warm, not-scary water jets shoot up from the ground from several places in the yard, offering a quick way to cool off. There are also rows of adjustable water cannons, so kids can either soak each other to the skin or hide behind a barrier to avoid the spray. A mock-up of a friendly fire engine offers more opportunity for imaginative play. On the opposite side of the yard is a covered area with colorful oversized blocks for crafting epic towers or other creative designs. When the weather turns cold and the water is turned off, the Fun Yard is still worthy of a stop to let the kids run around, climb, and build. Although there's not a lot of dedicated seating here, there are some low stone walls where you can sit while dispensing snacks or watching the kids play, but don't be afraid to join in yourself!

▶ Park Pointers

Because of its proximity to Wild Eagle, FireChaser Express, and Tennessee Tornado, use of this play area is convenient when the family needs to split up so that some folks can hop aboard rides the younger ones aren't able to enjoy yet. Firehouse Fun Yard is neighbor to Splinter's Funnel Cakes just across the way, so if you need to pick up a beverage, snack, or one of Dollywood's amazing funnel cakes while letting the kids play and taking a break yourself, this is a perfect time! In an area of the park that has more attractions for older kids and adults, keep this playground as a tool in your toolbox for ensuring that Dolly's youngest fans stay happy, cool, and entertained.

4. Handsville Wax Company

FAST FACTS

WHAT: Specialized shop creating detailed wax molds of your hands for a truly unique souvenir.

WHERE: Next to the funnel cake stand in Wilderness Pass. You'll see buckets full of water and basins of melted wax with wooden lids.

EXPERT TIP: If you're at Dollywood with someone special—a dear friend, family member, partner, or child—make a mold of your entwined hands for a one-of-a-kind keepsake.

▶ Why You Should See It

Dollywood has no lack of memorable souvenirs, and the custom-molded hand figures at Handsville Wax Company are just one more way to always remember your time in the Smokies. The process starts by choosing the hand shape you want preserved in wax. If dipping a single hand, you can make a "number one" finger sign or a peace sign, cross your fingers, splay all five fingers evenly, flash a rock and roll salute, or do whatever you want! Once you've chosen a pose, you'll be asked to dip your hand into a bucket of cool water before applying some lotion to assist with wax removal later in the process. Next, your ability to stay still will be put to the test as you strike your desired pose and repeatedly dip your hand in warm melted wax, allowing the layers to slowly build. Your Dollywood host will alternate your hand between the wax and the water and will assist with how long to dip in each bucket; your main job is keeping your hand as still as possible! Once the dipping is complete, the host will gently loosen the wax and slide your hand out, leaving a perfect likeness. Final touches are added while the wax is still warm, including smoothing out rough spots and creating a flat base so that the mold can stand upright. You'll have your choice of final, glossy colors to perfect your creation, and then the finished product will be set aside to dry. Oh, and don't limit yourself to single-handed sculptures: Include a loved one to commemorate your visit! Some ideas for two-handed dipping include holding hands in different ways (fingers interlocked, folded, etc.), forming a heart, or placing palms flat against each other. After getting it home safe and sound, your elegant sculpture will make you smile every time you see it perched on your shelf.

▶ Park Pointers

In addition to creating your own wax hands, you can also find wax-dipped roses, lilies, and tulips in a variety of colors, or you can add a rose or butterfly to your molded hand for a small extra fee. East Tennessee can get hot, really hot, especially during peak summer months. So it's not ideal to be carrying around a custom wax figure and risking it getting marred by the soaring temperatures. Handsville Wax Company takes advantage of Dollywood's Package Pickup service to keep your gift safe and sound at Dollywood Emporium when you're ready to exit the park.

 ### Dolly Has Her Own Wax Figure

Dolly has always joked that while she may look "fake" on the outside, she's all real on the inside. At the Hollywood Wax Museum in Pigeon Forge, however, you can see a version of Dolly that's *actually* fake, as the museum displays a full-sized likeness of the superstar, complete with a glitzy red outfit and big blond wig.

5. The Dog House

FAST FACTS

WHAT: Classic hot dog stand serving up Dollywood spins on a traditional theme park lunch.

WHERE: The no-frills stand is located across from the firefighter-themed souvenir shop in Wilderness Pass. The sign shaped like a hot dog tells you all you need to know.

EXPERT TIP: Give the French onion flavor a try—it's unique and fun!

▶ Why You Should See It

Grab-and-go snack stands like The Dog House are the primary dining options on the north side of the loop, and it makes sense with so many rip-roaring rides and coasters concentrated in this section of the park. At its core, the menu is simple: all-beef hot dogs in split-top New England–style buns. You can keep it simple and stop right there—maybe adding a squiggle of mustard or ketchup—or you can make things a little more interesting and choose one of the specialty topping combos from the menu board. The Tennessee Top Dog, with chili, cheese sauce, chopped onion, and bacon, is a tasty choice (just make sure to grab a bunch of napkins for this one!), while Firechaser Express Mac 'N' Cheese Dog will satisfy carb fans, piled high with white Cheddar macaroni and cheese. There are gluten-free buns and vegan franks available as well! If hot dogs aren't your thing, you can skip the frank altogether and order the brand-new pimento macaroni and cheese bread bowl with chili and onion, ooh la la!

▶ *Park Pointers*

During late spring and summer, there's a blue trailer parked next to The Dog House that sells mounds of finely shaved ice topped with flavored syrup. Orders are placed at The Dog House and then picked up at the trailer's front window. Cool off with your pick of twelve fun flavors like blue cotton candy, tiger's blood, green apple, and wedding cake. Add a drizzle of sweet cream or a "sour spray"—flavoring that'll make your shaved ice taste like your favorite gummy sour candy—and you'll be ready to roll. Cold treat, hot dog!

Dolly's Favorite Hot Dog

Speaking of hot dogs, one of Dolly's favorite local places to eat is Frank Allen's Market & Grill that's located inside a gas station in Sevierville. The unassuming eatery has been around since 1953, and Dolly always orders a "slaw dog"—a hot dog topped with coleslaw—whenever she visits.

6. Mystery Mine

WHAT: Intense roller coaster that sends you careening through an old, abandoned coal mine. Ride uses over-the-shoulder restraints, and riders must be at least 48 inches tall.

WHERE: The tracks cross the path overhead at the top of Timber Canyon, with the entrance to the queue located inside a rickety old mining company.

EXPERT TIP: You can get a great view while standing on the path underneath the 360-degree twisting portion of the track. If a member of your group is not riding, have them have a camera at the ready to get a video of you zooming by, or just be there to cheer you on!

▶ Why You Should See It

Before you jump into line to ride Dollywood's daring haunted coal mine coaster, stop and listen to Buzz the vulture just outside. Buzz will clue you in on the backstory behind Mystery Mine and the tale of Old Grandpa Jack. Jack had a talent for whistling, and one day while whistling in a cave—despite warnings that doing so could cause rocks to fall—the ground began to shake and a hole opened up, revealing a long-lost mine. Old Jack ran from the cave in fear, leaving his boots behind. Later, hoping to strike it rich with his discovery, Jack returned to the mine to get his boots but was never seen again.

Now it's your turn to explore the mine, bravely ignoring all the "danger" signs and newspaper clippings of past tragedies posted along the queue. At only two rows each, the mine carts provide equal opportunity for the "front row" experience. Because of the twists and inversions, you'll want to make sure that all loose items are secured, stored in lockers, or left with a non-rider.

Things get going right away as you are plunged into darkness as soon as the cart leaves the station. You then meander around a bit while suspiciously upbeat banjo music plays and the caws of crows (a bad omen inside a mine) can be heard and a canary in a cage seen. If you didn't know, canaries used to be kept in cages inside coal mines to monitor the air quality. If the canary stopped singing and dropped from its perch, it was a sign the miners needed to evacuate immediately. After a small drop and swerve in the darkness, the cart emerges into daylight and begins a steep 80-foot climb followed by a swift drop, a few quick hills, and an S curve before soaring right back into the building. After climbing a hill in the dark, you'll hear explosions as plumes of fire illuminate the dark hole in front of you. Before you can react, the cart plunges almost straight down the 85-foot shaft at 95 degrees, followed by a 360-degree twist (called a "heartline roll") and a harrowing dive loop before finally slowing down for its return to the station. Phew, you survived! Did you remember your boots?

▶ Park Pointers

April 13, 2007, marked the day that this hair-raising coaster was added to Dollywood's already impressive lineup of thrill rides. In 2021, the ride was updated to remove an over-banked curve and the 95-degree drop was modified. These changes made the ride no less scary but improved how smooth it felt. There is a test seat located outside, so if you have any comfort concerns with boarding the ride, you can take a seat and pull down the restraint to sense exactly how things will feel. Mystery Mine's track is both indoors and out, and the ride will close when there is lightning within 10 miles of the park, extreme precipitation, or high winds, or if the temperature drops below 34°F.

7. Lumberjack Lifts

══════ FAST FACTS ══════

WHAT: Self-operated rope lift ride that's not too high or scary. Uses lap bar and belt restraints. Riders must be at least 40 inches tall, and those under 48 inches must be accompanied by someone age 14 or older.

WHERE: Underneath the exterior tracks of Mystery Mine, you'll see the 30-foot towers and a sign for the queue hanging from a rope-lashed log frame.

EXPERT TIP: Make a bet with your friends on how many times you can make it up and down a tower during the ride.

▶ Why You Should See It

If you think that hiking around the park is all the exercise you're gonna get during a day at Dollywood, think again! Lumberjack Lifts will give your upper body a workout as you use a set of ropes to hoist your seat as high as 25 feet into the air. Riders sit as a pair, with single riders also allowed, and then are given free rein to ascend the tower as fast or as slow as they wish. The double seat has a rope in the middle that one or both riders can grasp and pull, pull, pull to rise into the air. When the rope is released, the chair descends in a controlled fall (not too fast) until it returns to the ground. There's no limit on how many times you can go up and down during the ride—which lets you play for about ninety seconds—so go hog wild until you can't go anymore. Winter is a great time to ride for one important reason: gloves! That rope can start to chafe after a few trips up the tower, so wearing gloves will help boost your stamina and prevent any pesky blisters from forming. Practically the whole family can enjoy Lumberjack Lifts, and considering it's surrounded by some big-time rides that may spook younger family members, it's a good way to take things down a notch.

▶ Park Pointers

Lumberjack Lifts joined Dollywood in 2006 and was a fitting addition to the "logging town" theme of Timber Canyon. The ride will close in either extreme hot or extreme cold temperatures, heavy precipitation, high winds, or when lightning strikes within 10 miles of the park. On the way down to the Lifts when coming from Mystery Mine, you'll pass by a couple of shopping opportunities: Wired Up Names and The Mine Shaft. At Wired Up Names, Dollywood artists use wire to twist and shape your scripted name into a beautiful piece of keepsake jewelry. The Mine Shaft also creates custom souvenirs in the form of personalized leather bracelets alongside branded Dollywood merchandise and souvenirs.

Dolly's Lumberjack Show

In 2015, Dolly announced that she had acquired the Lumberjack Feud Dinner Theater and planned to improve it for a grand reopening as Dolly Parton's Lumberjack Adventure. The new dinner-and-show venue was only open for a year before closing to be reimagined as Dolly Parton's Smoky Mountain Adventures, a story about Dolly's life and family. That show was also short-lived, and it closed only to be transformed into the current Pirates Voyage Dinner & Show.

8. Drop Line

WHAT: Colossal drop tower ride with the absolute best views in the whole park. Uses over-the-shoulder and belt restraints. Riders must be at least 55 inches tall.

WHERE: Sitting on its own island in the center of a small pond in Timber Canyon.

EXPERT TIP: Nervous? Don't try to resist or anticipate the fall—it can make the anxiety worse! Just take deep breaths, go with it, and scream your head off!

▶ Why You Should See It

If you want to see the most panoramic view of the park and the stunning Smoky Mountains, you'll have to brave the 230-foot plunge to the earth on Drop Line. This ride has the most stringent minimum height requirement in Dollywood, so only older children and grownups will be able to board. As the gondola slowly rises above the ground, it spins around the tower at a leisurely pace, giving you a full 360-degree view of Dollywood and the nearby triple peaks of Mount LeConte. Don't get too comfortable up there, though, because less than ten seconds after reaching the top you'll be hurtling down at speeds that'll leave your stomach somewhere behind. The accelerated fall at nearly 80 mph will hit with a force of negative

3.2 Gs, leaving you feeling weightless as the ground rushes up to meet you way faster than it seems it should. The plummet is over quickly, and before you know it you'll be standing up from your seat and walking on wobbly legs toward the ride exit. You're likely to have one of two thoughts upon completing a turn on Drop Line: you want to ride it again immediately, or you've seen enough of the panoramic view for one visit (or lifetime)!

▶ *Park Pointers*

Drop Line opened to visitors on May 6, 2017. It replaced the Timber Tower, a problematic Topple Tower ride that was closed after six years of operation. One notable issue with Timber Tower occurred on June 16, 2007, when a faulty safety sensor engaged, leaving riders stuck in the air for as many as six hours! After an accident on Orlando FreeFall, a drop tower in Florida by the same manufacturer as Drop Line, Dollywood closed the tower while safety investigations were conducted. The ride reopened nearly five months later with an increase of the minimum height requirement from 50 to 55 inches, a new safety belt between the legs, and a change to the ride cycle programming. Drop Line will close if temperatures drop to 5°F or below, in high winds, when lightning is detected within 10 miles of the park, or during heavy precipitation like rain, hail, or snow.

 ### Parent Swap

If you have members of your group who can't (or don't want to) experience certain attractions, take note! In line for any ride, tell the first host you see that you want to use Parent Swap. Everyone will go through the queue together, and then one parent waits with those who are not riding. Once the group of eligible children who are riding finishes, the parents swap, and those children get to ride again!

9. Lumber Jack's Pizza

============ FAST FACTS ============

WHAT: Personal-sized pizzas for fans of all things sauce-y, bread-y, and cheese-y.

WHERE: As the only place to get a meal in Timber Canyon, this pizza joint is located right across from the Drop Line pond.

EXPERT TIP: The Lumber Jack Pizza is a meat lover's dream.

▶ Why You Should See It

Pickin's are a bit slimmer on this side of the park when it comes to dining options, but Lumber Jack's Pizza serves up some solid pies, perfectly sized for a single person, to stave off the munchies while conquering Dollywood's biggest rides. Lumber Jack's previously sold giant individual slices of pizza, but later switched to the personal-sized model. With the newer menu, you can see what's available for the day by reading the menu board or looking inside the display case. Basic cheese and pepperoni pizzas are always hot and ready, and other styles come and go, such as The Lumber Jack—topped with sausage, pepperoni, and bacon—or Hawaiian-style for pineapple lovers. For those with certain dietary needs, Lumber Jack's is very accommodating, with a number of meatless vegan pizzas available each day, as well as gluten-free crust upon request. If you need some roughage, basic entrée salads can be purchased here. You can also find gluten-free brownies and prepackaged chocolate chip cookies (just be sure to save some room for the other dessert options in the park as well!).

A big draw of this location is the ease of finding covered seating—either under the pavilion or an umbrella—directly adjacent to the restaurant. The tables are across from the Drop Line pond, and you can have your lunch while enjoying the trickling sounds of water. During the fall, make sure to look for the adorable pumpkin-shaped frogs on lily pads, while during Christmas, watch for illuminated polar bears floating on big chunks of iceberg!

▶ Park Pointers

Being no stranger to giant food offerings with its famous 25-pound apple pie, Dollywood followed suit with its short-lived 12-pound pizza challenge at Lumber Jack's. The challenge included a 30-inch pizza absolutely loaded with toppings: pepperoni, chicken, sausage, and ham (not to mention the sauce and cheese, of course). If a maximum of three people ate all 12 pounds of pizza in one hour, the participants won a Super Gold season pass to Dollywood. There was also a "mini" version of the challenge with an 8-pound pizza and a maximum of two participants. For a time, a bulk recipe for Lumber Jack's wood-fired pizza dough—topped however you wanted—was posted on a chalkboard on the side of the building (psst... with some smart Internet searchin', you can still find the recipe to make at home and enjoy at your own pace).

Pizza...The Musical?

Dolly loves Mexican Pizzas from Taco Bell so much that she hopped onboard the marketing efforts of the fast-food chain when they announced the return of the beloved menu item in 2022 after a two-year absence. Dolly participated in *Mexican Pizza: The Musical*, a funny TikTok production to hype the pizza's return.

10. Whistle Punk Chaser

WHAT: Charming junior roller coaster with lap bar restraints. Riders must be at least 36 inches tall, and those under 42 inches must be accompanied by someone age 14 or older.

WHERE: The bright orange tracks of this mini steel coaster lie beneath the rumbles of the mighty Thunderhead coaster, reminding the kids what they're working toward!

EXPERT TIP: Despite being a kid-friendly coaster, this ride has some herky-jerky elements. Keep that in mind if your child is sensitive to sudden starts and stops.

▶ Why You Should See It

Think of Whistle Punk Chaser as a starter coaster before moving up the ranks to the monster tracks that Dollywood is known for. This adorable ride falls somewhere between a true "kiddie coaster" and a family coaster. Grownups are welcomed and encouraged to ride with their kids, but it is still very much a mild ride compared to the next step up in thrills like FireChaser Express. There's a spacious shady area next to the queue that's perfect for parking strollers or for non-riders to hang out and watch. If an adult is riding with a child, the child will be asked to sit in the inner seat. While there's no stated maximum size for riding Whistle Punk Chaser, the lap bar must be able to fully click into place before the ride can begin.

The train starts moving with a jerk before climbing the short chain lift hill. Three circuits of the 262.5-foot track are made, which include short drops and easy curves. Listen for the steam whistle to call out as you come around the last curve in each loop!

▶ Park Pointers

Whistle Punk Chaser has been drawing excited squeals from little folks since May 21, 2017. The name of this roller coaster comes from the combination of two traditional logging job titles, appropriate for the theming of Timber Canyon. A "whistle punk" acted as a communicator between the worker hooking up the logs to the transport system and the person controlling the movement of the logs. The job was an important one, since it helped ensure the safety of the other loggers when working with the massive trees. Fatalities and injuries in the industry were common! The whistle punk blew a series of whistle codes to alert the other members of the team about the current status of the log and whether to pull on it or not. A "chaser" was positioned at the delivery point to detach the choker—a noose of strong cable—from the log. Whistle Punk Chaser may close when any precipitation is present, during high winds or temperatures below 36°F, or when lightning is detected within 10 miles of the park.

Jammin'

At the top of the Timber Canyon hill, across from the entrance to the Whistle Punk ride queue, you can stop at Lumberjack Jam Band, a musical play area with primitive instruments like pots, pans, and a giant skillet.

11. Thunderhead

══ FAST FACTS ══

WHAT: Good old-fashioned wooden roller coaster with high speeds and huge drops. Uses lap bar and seat belt restraints. Riders must be at least 48 inches tall.

WHERE: This behemoth of a coaster wraps around the entire northern corner of Timber Canyon; the loud roar of the train can be heard from far away.

EXPERT TIP: Itching to get on a coaster as soon as possible? Thunderhead is the closest one to the park entrance. Turn left after entering the park and follow the tree-covered hill to the top and you'll be flying high in no time.

▶ Why You Should See It

Thunderhead is a masterpiece of engineering and a beautiful example of a classic wooden roller coaster. The character of this rugged ride fits right in with the mountainous tree-covered setting, and it'll be a ride you won't soon forget. When the train leaves the station, it takes a right turn and immediately begins the climb up the tall chain lift hill. After reaching the crest, it zooms down 100 feet and straight into a sharp curve before shooting you up a hill and sending you flailing back down again. By now, there will be no question that you're on a wooden roller coaster, because the train will be bellowing down the track at speeds of 55 mph. You'll feel your rear end lift out of the seat more than once, and a few of those swift turns and hills will have you wondering if you're actually going to take off and fly. Hopefully you like the person you're riding next to, because the banks on Thunderhead will likely have you bumping shoulders as you're tossed to and fro in your seat. The track crosses over (and under) itself thirty-two times and is representative of Great Coasters International's super-twisty styes of wooden coasters.

▶ Park Pointers

The impressive Thunderhead coaster—Dollywood's first of its type—welcomed riders starting on April 3, 2004, in an area of the park carved out of the hillside and known as Thunderhead Gap. To construct the sprawling 3,230-foot track, contractors used 700,000 feet of Southern yellow pine; 3,600 yards of concrete; 250,000 bolts; 185,000 feet of steel rebar; and 2 *million* screws! Can you imagine how much it must weigh? Even after this coaster's over twenty years in service, Dollywood keeps it (and all the rides in the park) in tip-top shape. It takes six hours to inspect every square inch of the track, and every single one of those bolts mentioned previously is tightened at least once per season. The chains that pull the train up the hill get a refresh every six to eight seasons, and the original pine track has been updated gradually since 2018 with an incredibly strong Brazilian hardwood that has resulted in a smoother ride. Thunderhead will close when lightning is detected within 10 miles of the park, during high winds or heavy precipitation, or when temperatures drop below 34°F. Dollywood warns of possible bee and wasp swarms near the highest parts of the ride during spring and fall.

A Rare Maneuver

Thunderhead's track contains a fly-through station element where the train passes through the station on a portion of the track not used for loading or unloading.

CHAPTER EIGHT

Wildwood Grove

★ ★

Wildwood Grove is the most recent expansion to Dollywood, and boy is it a doozy! Straight out of Dolly Parton's childhood dreams of setting off into the great outdoors and exploring nature, this area combines Smoky Mountain beauty with whimsical fantasy in a land filled with butterflies, bees, frogs, and friendly black bears. As you explore, the sounds of fountains, rocky creeks, and waterfalls are a relaxing soundtrack to go along with the fanciful vibe. Full of good food, rides both gentle and thrilling, and play areas for the little ones, Wildwood Grove provides diverse opportunities that'll have the whole family enjoying themselves.

WILDWOOD GROVE

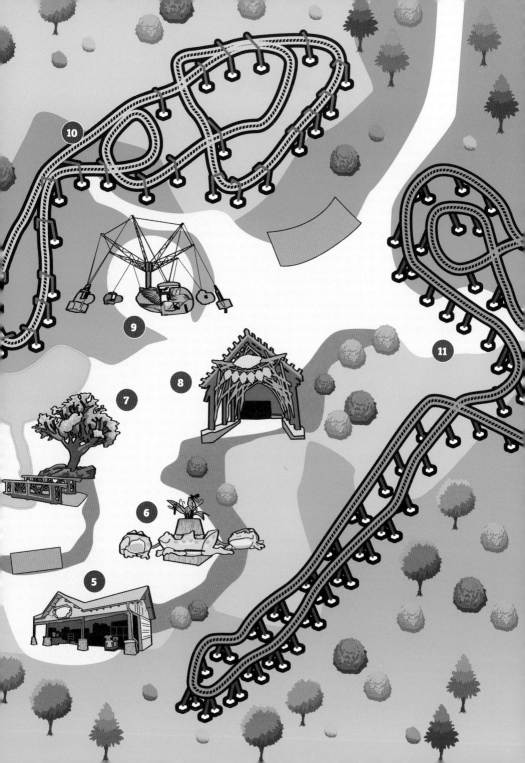

1. Till & Harvest Food Hall

WHAT: Large cafeteria-style Mexican and American eatery with tons of covered seating; the primary restaurant in Wildwood Grove.

WHERE: When you pass through the larger-than-life hollow tree entrance into Wildwood Grove, this restaurant is on your right, next to a musical fountain.

EXPERT TIP: The menu changes often. Check online (or call) before you go if you're trying to preplan your meals and make sure they have what you like!

▶ Why You Should See It

Till & Harvest Food Hall is where you'll find the most substantial, filling meals in Dollywood's Wildwood Grove expansion. The restaurant's outdoor menu board describes the establishment's offerings as "Smoky Mountain Mexican." Initially, the restaurant used a build-your-own bowl or burrito system. You'd choose a tortilla or a base (rice or cheese grits) and then load it up with beans, chicken, steak, pork, pico de gallo, onions, peppers, cheese sauces, and more. The establishment stuck with this style for a couple of years before switching to a selection of tasty premade dishes with the same quick counter service. More recent items seen on the menu include a black bean taco–stuffed sweet potato, Smoky Mountain Nachos, cilantro lime chicken and rice, guajillo beef mac and cheese, and Mexican street corn kale salad topped with grilled chicken. On the American side of the menu, there are hamburgers, cheeseburgers, and chicken tenders, all served with crinkle-cut French fries or a selection of kettle-cooked potato chips. Till & Harvest fills a delicious niche by adding some Mexican tastes to a theme park that already has "Southern and deep-fried" well covered.

▶ Park Pointers

Afternoon thunderstorms are a common sight in East Tennessee, and because Dollywood takes safety seriously, most of the rides close down when lightning strikes near the park. This happens more often during the spring and summer months. When rain starts to fall, people head for any indoor attraction or covered space they can find to avoid getting drenched. The large seating pavilion next to Till & Harvest is a good place to keep an eye on the weather and stay dry while still being able to enjoy the smell of rain in the Smoky Mountains. Folks who live in this area have to learn to roll with the punches when it comes to weather and not see the rain as a hindrance but more as...just a part of life.

 ### Sweets and Treats

Looking for a little dessert after your meal? Next to Till & Harvest, you'll find a small walk-up spot where you can get churros, a waffle cone shaped like a bear (very fitting), and other sweets, as well as soda floats to wash everything down.

2. Treetop Tower

WHAT: Family-friendly gondola ride that sends you aboard twirling acorns that climb the trunk of an "oak tree" tower. Uses seat belt restraints, and riders under 42 inches must be accompanied by someone age 14 or older.

WHERE: This is the first ride straight ahead as you enter Wildwood Grove. Hard to miss it!

EXPERT TIP: Dizziness warning! If you get motion sickness easily, sit this one out.

▶ Why You Should See It

With no minimum or maximum height restrictions, Treetop Tower welcomes everyone from babies to grandma. A Samba Tower ride by manufacturer Zamperla using their popular balloon gondolas, this ride type is often seen in family attractions and makes a big impact without taking up a ton of space. Each ride circuit can hold about thirty-two people (depending on age and size), so even if there's a line, it'll move quickly. The queue area is shady and dry, so any wait you do have is relatively comfortable. Once you are tucked inside your "acorn," the gondola starts to rotate as it climbs to the top of the (not too tall) tower. Round and round you go, and while you get a nice view of this corner of Wildwood Grove and a bit of Timber Canyon down the hill, you might be spinning a little too fast to really take in the details. There's a pole in the middle of each compartment to hold on to if you feel the need, but you won't experience any intense forces on this ride. The diameter of the circle made by the acorns is not very big, so you'll complete a whole lotta trips around the tower before returning to the ground. These multiple rotations can mess with your equilibrium even though the ride is overall mild and slow. If you feel yourself getting woozy from inside your acorn, focus your gaze down at your feet or on the knees of the person sitting across from you. Not being able to see the world whizzing by outside will help your system steady itself. If you find yourself needing to splash some cold water on your face, though, the ride is conveniently located next to large public restroom facilities so everyone can get a bathroom break before heading off to the next fun spot.

▶ Park Pointers

When Dolly was telling the public how the theme of Wildwood Grove came about, she explained that when you're proud of where you came from, you want to share that with the world. That's what she has done with the aesthetic of Wildwood Grove, sharing what it was like for her growing up in the mountains, wrapped in nature and combining imagination with the preexisting wonder of the outdoor world. When browsing through the area, take note of how each attraction fits with the theme. Treetop Tower, with its autumn-colored oak leaves and giant swirling acorns, may remind you of playing under the trees as a child or of turning acorns into funny characters wearing "nutty" hats. Treetop Tower will close during high winds, heavy precipitation, or temperatures below 32°F, and when lightning is detected within 10 miles of the park.

3. Great Tree Swing

FAST FACTS

WHAT: Swinging "pirate ship" ride with lap bar restraints. Riders must be at least 36 inches tall to ride, and anyone under 48 inches must be accompanied by someone age 14 or older.

WHERE: Across from the roaring waterfall under the orange tracks of Big Bear Mountain.

EXPERT TIP: For the tamest ride, sit near the center of the swing. For the wildest ride, sit in the very front or the very back.

▶ Why You Should See It

Fly through the trees with the greatest of ease on Dollywood's Great Tree Swing. Legend has it that the mighty swing was constructed from the gigantic leaves and vines of the magical Wildwood Tree. You can choose your seat along the large, curved boat-shaped swing, and a lap bar is clicked into place once you're settled. Things start out nice and easy with a few low and slow back-and-forths. After a few swings, you start going faster and higher...but how high? At this point, you're probably feeling some little flutters in your tummy when the movement reaches its most intense. You might even start to feel lifted out of your seat briefly. Make sure to peep at the tracks of nearby Thunderhead and Dragonflier—you'll have a great view! As the ride starts to slow down and eventually comes to a stop, let yourself feel both relief and accomplishment knowing you've swung through the trees of Wildwood Grove. This fun twist on an amusement park classic appeals to both thrill seekers and those looking for a bit of excitement in a family-friendly setting.

▶ *Park Pointers*

In the early days after the Wildwood Grove expansion was announced, initial concept art was released showing a colorful illustration of this ride with its original name: Sycamore Swing. The design stayed largely the same, including the art depicting the large autumn-colored leaves, vine-wrapped swing, and friendly critters that were eventually brought to life when the ride was finally built. If you need to stop and rest for a moment after your ride, just up the path near where Wildwood Creek crosses underneath a low bridge you'll find some covered seating areas with fans. Great Tree Swing will close when any kind of precipitation is present, and also during high winds or temperatures below 32°F, and when lightning is detected within 10 miles of the park.

Love Is Like a Butterfly

Dolly released *Love Is Like a Butterfly*, her fourteenth solo studio album, in 1974. There was a track on the album with the same title, and for the official launch event for Wildwood Grove, she rewrote the lyrics to include all the new rides and other elements in the area. She performed the song wearing a sparkly purple and silver butterfly outfit (of course!).

4. Black Bear Trail

═ FAST FACTS ═

WHAT: Slow-moving, frolicking black bear ride with belt restraints. Riders must be at least 36 inches tall to ride, and anyone under 42 inches must be accompanied by someone age 14 or older.

WHERE: You'll find these adorable big-eyed bears traipsing among the flowers and streams on the corner of the large central area in Wildwood Grove.

EXPERT TIP: Have a non-rider stand in the garden area in the middle of the track for the perfect vantage point to take a photo of those riding the bears!

▶ Why You Should See It

The most pleasant, easy ride in Wildwood Grove, Black Bear Trail is just as cute as it can be. After working your way through the covered switchback queue, you climb aboard your "bear" and snap the seat belt into place. Riders who are tall enough can ride alone, or an adult or teenager can ride with a smaller child; the seat belt extends to fit across both riders in that case. The bears are styled like Benjamin Bear, a new jolly roaming character you might see wandering around outside. With their big green eyes and necklace fashioned out of vines and leaves, these charming bears are nothing to fear. When your bear sets off, there's a small acceleration, and then you'll settle into a rhythmic trot as you make your way around and through the winding garden. You'll hear the cheery music of Wildwood Grove emanating from hidden speakers, and you might hear the buzzing of a few bees as well (but don't worry, they're not real!). The bears are spaced out well, so there's a sense of solitude as you ride. If you're riding with your little one, this is a perfect memory-making experience as the two of you chitchat and point out the pretty surroundings. The ride is simple to board and exit, though you will have to step up onto the bear and swing your leg over its back, kind of like climbing onto a bike. Just keep in mind that loading and unloading can be slow, so the line takes a while to get through if it's a crowded day. Plan accordingly.

▶ *Park Pointers*

Black Bear Trail is a "pony trek" ride by German manufacturer Metallbau Emmeln, so if the movement of the bear sort of feels like a galloping horse, that's why! Dolly's vision that Wildwood Grove manifests a carefree child following creatures and critters off into the woods is perfectly represented by this attraction. So climb aboard, hold on tight, and enjoy the ride! Black Bear Trail will close when there is heavy precipitation or lightning detected within 5 miles of the park, or during *super*-cold days that are 23°F or below.

Too Close for Comfort

When Dolly was growing up in her little cabin back in the holler, she was no stranger to the sight of the black bears that call the Smoky Mountains their home. Some of those bears were so curious that they would end up right in her backyard!

5. Mountain Grove Merchants

WHAT: Small retail hot spot for basic necessities and Wildwood Grove souvenirs.

WHERE: This open-air (but covered) shop is located right between a sleuth of bears and an army of frogs—the rides that employ those creatures, that is!

EXPERT TIP: Did you forget something for your trip to Dollywood? Perhaps sunscreen or a pair of sunglasses? Find those and more supplies right here.

▶ Why You Should See It

The merchandise in the shop fits with the woodsy, natural theme of Wildwood Grove. The shelves have fun souvenirs you can't find anywhere else in the park. You may see things like coppery coffee mugs and glass water bottles; wood-burned magnets and key chains; and all kinds of hats, T-shirts, and other apparel. Everything for sale perpetuates the message of using your imagination to explore the natural world. Butterflies, fireflies, dragonflies, and images of the iconic Wildwood Tree are just some of the symbols you'll see. Sometimes, you can find little pairs of sparkly wings to gift the fledgling butterflies in your party. You can even create your own Grove necklace by choosing a necklace cord, beads, and charm for a souvenir that is all for you, made by you! The shop is conveniently located just before you reach some of the more intense rides in Wildwood Grove, like Big Bear Mountain, The Mad Mockingbird, and Dragonflier, so those who aren't into thrills can wait here for a little browsing to fill some of the time.

▶ Park Pointers

When Dollywood designers were planning Mountain Grove Merchants, they wanted to bring in a real tree to place right inside the shop. Out into the woods they went in search of the absolutely perfect tree to serve as the natural centerpiece of this cozy little spot. They scored big-time when they found a beautiful tree with a graceful curve and three large branches splaying out from the trunk. While cutting down the tree and readying it to move to Dollywood, one of the large branches snapped off. The tree was used anyway, after being wrapped in vines and colorful leaves. The broken branch was salvaged and hidden as part of the decor in Till & Harvest Food Hall—see if you can find it!

Why So Many Butterflies?

Butterflies are seen all over this shop, and all over Dollywood! Why so many? The gentleness of butterflies is a draw for the music star. They don't sting or bite, they're beautiful, and Dolly relates to them. After adopting them as her own personal symbol, Dolly has incorporated butterflies into almost everything she does.

6. Frogs & Fireflies

WHAT: Kiddie ride with lively bouncing frogs that uses belt restraints. No minimum height requirement, though riders under 36 inches tall must be accompanied by someone age 14 or older.

WHERE: Listen for the *boing-boing* sounds and watch for the big green frogs going around in a circle just past the main gift shop in Wildwood Grove.

EXPERT TIP: If you have a nervous child who isn't sure about riding, a grownup can sit in the back seat for reassurance.

▶ Why You Should See It

Climb aboard the back of a ravenous amphibian and hang on tight while it jumps and bounces to score some delicious fireflies. No big scares to worry about here; this is a cute ride that the littles will love. The queue for this ride is located opposite the main path, so you can allow older children to go through the line alone (preferably with a sibling or buddy). You are then able to keep a close eye on them from the main path without worrying that they'll dart away from the attraction. Once riders are seated and buckled up, a Dollywood ride host comes around to make sure everyone is safe and secured. As the ride starts, the frogs lift off the ground all at the same time. They won't go too high, though; their ascent stops only a couple of feet aboveground. As the frogs start to bound around the tall grass at the center, small bounces combined with a few more-pronounced leaps will keep everyone giggling. Giant twinkling fireflies hover just above the grass, and sadly, just out of reach of the desperate frogs. Spoiler alert: The poor frogs don't ever catch their tasty treat, but that won't stop the kids from wanting to ride again and again to see if one time, just once, they might.

▶ *Park Pointers*

Frogs & Fireflies is a themed Jump Around ride by manufacturer Zamperla. The ride can hold four children per frog, two per row, or one adult with two children. This ride is a great choice for kids who have graduated from the rides in Happy Valley Farmyard and want to take a teeny step up toward bigger rides. It's still a nice and easy ride with a tad more thrill than the most basic kiddie rides. Frogs & Fireflies will close when there is high wind, heavy precipitation, or lighting within 5 miles of the park, or when the temperatures drop to a chilly 32°F.

Dancing Fireflies

Dolly has a line of well-reviewed fragrances—the glass bottles are each topped with a crystal butterfly—and one of her signature scents is Dancing Fireflies. It's a light, casual scent with top notes of pink apple, heart notes of pink peonies, and base notes of pink musk. Four other fragrances are in the collection: Scent From Above, Early Morning Breeze, Smoky Mountain, and Tennessee Sunset.

7. The Wildwood Tree

WHAT: Butterfly-laden tree towering over Wildwood Grove, surrounded by a fun water play area. Comes to life at night!

WHERE: The majestic tree is positioned at the end of Wildwood Creek. Look up and see how many butterflies you can count!

EXPERT TIP: The evening light and projection shows change through the years, so stop by often to see them all!

▶ Why You Should See It

Dolly's favorite addition to Wildwood Grove is the majestic Wildwood Tree that stands as the crown jewel of the area. At the official media launch event, she said that if she had the tree in her yard at home, she'd add a ladder, a tree house, and a swing to really make good use of it. The former president of The Dollywood Company, Craig Ross, described the tree as a representation of the heart of Dolly Parton and her childhood memories. The great hardwood rises 50 feet above Wildwood Grove, providing shade with its 9,000 artificial leaves and more than 600 acrylic butterflies. The butterflies twinkle and shimmer in a gradient of colors, so don't miss strolling through at night when the beauty of the tree is at its most impressive. Evening is also when you can catch the looping light show on the tree as the butterflies twinkle in synchronization to music and Dolly herself narrates a story about the legend of the tree. Listen as she explains how at night, when the Grove comes alive, dreams can come true through the power of love and light. While the story is being told, leaves, vines, and more butterflies in flight are projected onto the trunk and base of the tree, changing along with the music. If you're walking down Timber Canyon at night on your way out of the park at the end of your visit, it's worth taking the detour to Wildwood Grove to let the animated illuminations leave you with one last magical memory of the park.

▶ Park Pointers

When the weather is warm, the area surrounding the base of The Wildwood Tree turns into a mini splash pad with family-friendly fountains and pop jets for keeping cool. At the end of Wildwood Creek, you can kick off your shoes and roll up your pants legs before wading and splashing in the shallow, sparkling water. Low stone walls surround the mini plaza where you can rest after cooling your heels. Nearby, a collection of fun instruments sits ready to create music. Oversized chimes, xylophones, and drums add rhythm to the cadence of the trickling creek. Keep your camera at the ready, because you'll want to capture a memory or two with the creek and grand Wildwood Tree as your backdrop.

The Partons' First TV

Dolly put her tree-climbing skills to good use when, as a 10-year-old, she entered a greasy pole climbing contest at a Sevierville theater. The prize was a sum of money affixed to the top of the pole. Before climbing, she rolled around in the dirt and gravel to help create friction. She nabbed the prize money at the top and used it to buy her family's first TV set.

8. Hidden Hollow

WHAT: Massive climate-controlled indoor play area with dim lighting and comfortable seating.

WHERE: Inside the large building across from the twirling Mad Mockingbird ride. You'll likely see a bunch of strollers parked outside.

EXPERT TIP: This is the *best* playground in Dollywood, so if you have to choose just one to visit...choose this one!

▶ Why You Should See It

It's easy to miss the entrance to Hidden Hollow, since it's hard to tell exactly what lies within from the humble branch-covered porch in front of the sizable building. If you are spending a day at Dollywood with kids, this is one attraction you absolutely, no buts about it, have to know about. When you walk inside for the first time—after letting your eyes adjust to the relaxing dim lighting in contrast to the glaringly sunny day you likely entered from—your jaw will drop. To your right, you'll see a set of cubbies for shoes and jackets. Stop there first. Once you've stowed away their items, let the kids run wild. No matter where you sit, you can easily keep an eye on them through the mesh safety barricades that enclose the play structures. There's a special toddler area for younger kids to enjoy safely with smaller structures and shorter "ladders" to climb. In the main area, kids can climb stairs, ramps, and nets to encounter fun challenges like rope crossings, wobble poles, and lookout windows that provide a view of the entire place. A triple-lane wavy slide offers a quick return to the ground floor. The Smoky Mountain wooded theme is apparent in the glowing tree trunks painted on the walls and the Mason jars, reminiscent of securing twinkling fireflies, hanging from the tall ceilings. The whole place evokes the ambience of a country evening at dusk and is a truly amazing addition to the park.

▶ Park Pointers

Since Hidden Hollow is a safe, fully enclosed area, go ahead and take a rest while your kids go nuts until they just can't anymore. There is cushioned seating along the side wall and in the center of the play area, as well as chargers in the wall for juicing up devices. If you have a child with physical limitations that prevent climbing, there are accessible activities on the ground level to enjoy, like an infinity floor and a running-in-place racing game that sends lights up a pole. Hidden Hollow is not a childcare center, so someone age 14 or older will need to be present in the building at all times. Because the play area is completely indoors, weather conditions will not affect its operation. Seeking shelter here on a yucky day is nice, but keep in mind that many other folks probably have the same idea, so expect more of a crowd. Bad weather days also send Flit, Flutter, and Benjamin Bear—Wildwood Grove's wandering characters—into the Hollow for their meet-and-greet photo ops, so if they're not wandering around outside, they're probably in here.

9. The Mad Mockingbird

WHAT: A medium-thrills ride with seat belt restraints. Riders must be at least 36 inches tall, and those under 48 inches must be accompanied by someone age 14 or older.

WHERE: You'll find the blue structure of this attraction whirling around just before you get to the green tracks of the Dragonflier roller coaster.

EXPERT TIP: Feeling nervous? Keep your "mockingbird" steady by holding on tight to the rudder handle and maintaining it in one position. This will prevent the vast majority of twisting and jerking and give you a smoother ride.

▶ Why You Should See It

As the state bird of Tennessee, there is no lack of real mockingbirds flying around Dollywood, so it makes sense that Wildwood Grove would have its own mockingbird-themed ride. Though mockingbirds in the wild sport only gray and white feathers, the birds on The Mad Mockingbird come in all sorts of colors. Two riders can fit side by side in each bird, and there's a handle in the center that acts as a rudder and turns the "head" left or right. Once everyone is tucked inside with seat belts fastened, the birds will start to rotate around the center post. Centrifugal force pushes the birds outward as the speed increases. Here's where you have a choice. Grab on to that handle and experiment with turning the rudder to torque. If you're a seasoned daredevil and want to show off, try varying the direction of the rudder so that your bird goes a little berserk, flying up high, then almost stalling out at lower points. Make sure you're riding with someone who agrees with how intensely to swivel your bird, though, so that no one is surprised or scared by sudden twisting!

▶ Park Pointers

The Mad Mockingbird is a Flying Scooters ride by Larson International. The rides were originally manufactured in the 1930s and 1940s by Bisch Rocco, based in Chicago, Illinois. The concept became insanely popular due to the ride being relatively inexpensive and even transportable for traveling fairs. As the new millennium approached, the rides started falling out of fashion, with many of the original Bisch Rocco models closing down. In the early 2000s, Larson International brought the ride back to life with a version that was only for permanent installments. In the early 2010s, Larson partnered with Majestic Manufacturing to design a version of the modern Flying Scooter that could be transported. The newer Larson models were designed to prevent "snapping," or jerking of the cables supporting the ride vehicles when a rider operates the rudder in a way that causes erratic movement for a more intense experience. Due to safety and maintenance concerns that come about as a result of snapping, attempting the stunt is frowned upon and strongly discouraged. The Mad Mockingbird will close when lightning is detected within 10 miles of the park and during high winds.

 ### Mockingbird Sings

In 2013, Dolly recorded a duet with fiddler Stuart Duncan called "Listen to the Mockingbird." The song, written in 1855 by Septimus Winner and Richard Milburn, was used as marching music during the Civil War. The track appeared on a compilation album of Civil War–era music titled *Divided & United*.

10. Dragonflier

FAST FACTS

WHAT: Suspended steel roller coaster that transforms you into a dragonfly riding the breeze. Uses a pull-down lap bar and a between-the-legs belt. Riders must be between 39 and 81 inches tall to ride, and those under 48 inches must be accompanied by someone age 14 or older.

WHERE: Head toward the bright green tracks at the bottom corner of Wildwood Grove to reach the entrance to the queue.

EXPERT TIP: To squeeze the most intensity out of Dragonflier, try to sit in the back row. You'll feel like you are being thrown over the top of that first hill, phew!

▶ Why You Should See It

Once you've reached this part of Wildwood Grove, you've already been a leaf blowing in the wind, rode on a black bear, hopped along with frogs, and taken flight with mockingbirds. Now things get a little more daring as you embark on your next adventure: experiencing the unpredictable maneuvers of an East Tennessee dragonfly. Dragonflies in the wild are known for their darting flight patterns and sudden change of direction, and Dollywood's Dragonflier will send you on a journey that is darn close to the real thing. Your feet are hanging free once you're secured into your seat, and when the train leaves the station and takes a sharp left turn, you begin to climb the friction wheel lift hill into the most intense portion of the ride right out of the gate! After plunging down a 63-foot drop through an underground tunnel, you emerge back into daylight and race uphill into a sharp curve that almost—but not quite—takes you upside down. After that, swing your feet, throw your head back, and enjoy the rest of your flight as you dip and swerve through a series of maneuvers that are more fun than frightening. You reach a top speed of just over 46 mph and experience close encounters with nearby plants and a fountain spurting up from a stone pond. Before you know it, the train is slowing to a stop back at the station, with the entire ride lasting for only one minute.

▶ Park Pointers

If you're able to ride FireChaser Express with no problem, this coaster is the next one to have on your radar. Aside from that first steep drop and the near-inversion right afterward, you'll find the rest of the coaster pretty gentle. The ride offers a chance to flirt with inversions without actually going all the way upside down, making it a perfect stepping stone to the bigger roller coasters in Dollywood. With a low height requirement, most of the family can enjoy this ride without finding it too scary. Dragonflier will close during high winds or heavy precipitation, when lightning is detected within 10 miles of the park, or when temperatures reach 36°F or below.

 ### A New President

As president of The Dollywood Company for over a decade, Craig Ross worked closely with Dolly, known as the "Dreamer in Chief," to bring massive growth to the park. After overseeing the $37 million Wildwood Grove expansion and navigating Dollywood through the early days of the COVID-19 pandemic, he passed the torch in 2020 to Eugene Naughton, who became the company's third president.

11. Big Bear Mountain

FAST FACTS

WHAT: Sprawling steel roller coaster with lap bar restraints. Riders must be at least 39 inches tall, and those under 38 inches must be accompanied by someone age 14 or older.

WHERE: Though you can see the bright orange steel tracks winding their way along the entire length of Wildwood Grove, the entrance to the ride queue is tucked into the farthest corner of the area.

EXPERT TIP: As it's Dollywood's newest major ride, expect lines to be long on crowded days. Visit when schools are in session and shoot for midweek (Wednesday or Thursday) for less congestion.

► Why You Should See It

When springtime of 2023 hit (Wildwood Grove's fourth season in operation), Dollywood opened its tenth roller coaster, Big Bear Mountain. The multilaunch coaster fills the gap between milder family coasters (think FireChaser Express and Dragonflier) and the big boys (think Thunderhead all the way up to Lightning Rod). The theme is captivating as you join Ned Oakley—experienced wilderness explorer (and fictional character)—on his endless search for proof of the existence of Big Bear, a legendary mammal that's been leaving behind clues of his presence since 1894. As you go through the queue—decked out as Adventure Outpost Base Camp—you'll learn more about ol' Big Bear, along with a map marked with alleged sightings throughout Dollywood along with blurry photos reminiscent of those of Big Foot. Take the time to stop and peruse the newspaper clippings, handwritten accounts, and sketches of historical sightings. Keep an eye out for a bear-related pun or two for a giggle before your trek.

Once you're seated and secure, be ready, because the coaster cars launch out of the station with gusto, hot on Big Bear's tail. The cars—designed to look like 4×4 off-road vehicles—have working headlights and audio narration that comes from speakers located between each pair of seats. Listen to Ned shout directions while you zoom through a second launch to pick up speed and make it through some tight turns. Things get really exciting when the cars zip right underneath a waterfall (don't worry, you won't get wet). Listen closely...was that a sinister growl you just heard? After more dips and curves, you hit the last launch in a final burst of speed. Proof of Big Bear is near! After a nearly two-minute wild ride, your cart brakes into the station. Phew, you're safe, and Ned is pretty sure you just saw Big Bear. Maybe next time you'll get some hard proof.

▶ Park Pointers

Big Bear Mountain is Dollywood's longest coaster at 3,990 feet. That's three-quarters of a mile! It's also the park's first ride with onboard audio, and the narration and suspenseful music add an extra level of immersion to the whole experience. There are few places in Wildwood Grove where you can't see the brightly colored track and rugged ride vehicles traipsing through the wilderness. Though much of the track dips low to the ground, the coaster reaches a height of 66 feet and a top speed of 48 mph. Not only is the ride's size impressive, but also its cost. Priced at $25 million, the coaster is the largest investment in a single attraction in the park's entire history. Big Bear Mountain will close during high winds and heavy precipitation, when lightning is detected within 10 miles of the park, and when the temperature drops below 36°F.

CHAPTER NINE

Festivals

Dollywood's festivals are a year-round party! Each season brings a new reason to celebrate at the park. Songwriting is celebrated during the I Will Always Love You Music Festival when the season kicks off in the spring. Next, things get flavorful and colorful with the Flower & Food Festival, followed by the Smoky Mountain Summer Celebration cooling down the hot months. When fall hits, the Harvest Festival floods the park with autumnal hues and warm flavors. The magical Smoky Mountain Christmas ends the year with sparkle and cheer, so as you can see, there's always something exciting happening. With peppy parades, tasty treats, themed live entertainment, and eye-popping decor, these festivals offer an ever-changing atmosphere that's perfect for anyone looking to have a blast.

1. I Will Always Love You Music Festival

FAST FACTS

WHAT: Dollywood's celebration of the art of storytelling through songwriting.

WHERE: Pink marks the spot, especially in the form of butterflies and sequins. So wherever you see pink, you'll find festival fun.

EXPERT TIP: Sign up for an I Will Always Love You walking tour. For a fee, this tour features ninety minutes of meet and greets, exclusive snacks, a special gift, and lots of fun insider information!

▶ Why You Should See It

This festival was, at first, only supposed to be a one-time deal. After its debut in March 2023, it was such a hit that park administrators quickly announced that the I Will Always Love You Music Festival would stake its claim as an annual celebration, filling in the open spot at the beginning of the season. Named after one of Dolly's biggest hits, the I Will Always Love You Music Festival was created to celebrate the fiftieth anniversary of Dolly putting these iconic lyrics to paper. The festival pays homage to songwriting with an entire lineup of shows at both indoor and outdoor theaters in the park. At Back Porch Theater's *Sing-a-long with Dolly* show, you can warm up your own vocal cords by belting out your favorite Dolly tunes! And at DP's Celebrity Theater, you can see *From the Heart: The Life and Music of Dolly Parton*. Debuting in

2024, this production showcases Dolly look-alike performers singing songs from her earliest days as a performer to her more modern hits.

Now let's talk about the food! During its first year, the festival exclusives were simple and few. Spotlight Bakery produced a vanilla Celebration Cupcake with pink sanding sugar and chocolate musical notes, while across the path at Sweet Shoppe Candy Kitchen you could try a piece of Songwriter fudge made of milk and white chocolates. When the 2024 season rolled around, a proper Tasting Pass became available, as well as an entire spread of sweet and savory goodies. The bakery expanded its festival menu to include pink velvet and white chocolate strawberry cupcakes and strawberry cannoli. The ice cream shop offers strawberry cheesecake milkshakes and raspberry cookies and cream—a sugar cookie topped with vanilla ice cream, raspberry crunch and coulis, whipped cream, and white chocolate sauce. The seasonal food booths are also full of mouthwatering items like jumbo baked potatoes loaded with turkey pot roast and gravy, smoked barbecue pork, or spinach and artichoke dip. As for beverages, guests can warm up with a luxurious peanut butter hot chocolate or hot cranberry tea, or cool down with a cup of I Will Always Love You Punch, which is a pineapple lemonade spritz. Funnel cakes are never left out of the festival fun, and the colorful strawberry cheesecake crunch funnel cake fits right in with the pink-packed theme.

▶ Park Pointers

Dolly recorded "I Will Always Love You" in 1973, and then released it a year later as a single. Dolly wrote the song as a loving goodbye to her business partner, Porter Wagoner, when she decided to pursue her own career. It reached the No. 1 spot on the US *Billboard* Hot Country Songs chart twice: once in 1974 and once in 1982. Despite the single's success on the charts, it was Whitney Houston's cover version in 1992 for the film *The Bodyguard* that *really* skyrocketed the song's popularity. Dolly has always raved about Houston's version of the song and has gone as far as calling it Houston's song. Nowadays there are a lot of folks who don't know that Dolly was the song's original performer as well as writer, but naming a whole festival after it should remedy that!

2. Flower & Food Festival

FAST FACTS

WHAT: Witness the park come alive with appreciation and celebration of the colors, blooms, and tastes of a Smoky Mountain springtime.

WHERE: Each area of the park offers something new to explore! This fragrant and flavorful festival spreads to every corner of Dollywood.

EXPERT TIP: Purchase a Tasting Pass (available during all five festivals at Dollywood), which allows you to sample up to five festival dishes for a great price!

▶ Why You Should See It

Dollywood's Flower & Food Festival is a radiant mecca for both flower and food enthusiasts alike. Living sculptures referred to as Mosaicultures, made from green plants and sprays of flowers, adorn the thoroughfares of the park. From oversized acrylic monarch butterflies to iconic Dolly Parton–inspired displays, you'll find yourself in a garden wonderland. In addition to taking photos of fantastic flora, you must snap a selfie beneath Showstreet's Umbrella Sky: a canopy of color spanning the buildings along the street, made up of hundreds of umbrellas. The umbrellas, which take three overnight shifts to hang, are a visual spectacle at the festival every year. Along with static displays, dynamic entertainment is going on as well, like energetic "living flower" street performers, special musical guests, and immersive experiences where guests can interact with motion-activated digital butterflies.

Now let's talk about the food, because you're in for a taste extravaganza! Imagine savoring mouthwatering treats that are not just delicious but also Instagram-worthy. From zesty, spice-packed dishes to sweet, melt-in-your-mouth desserts, the festival is a food lover's paradise. Sink your teeth into eats like garlic shrimp mac and cheese, beef bulgogi nachos, honey garlic chicken, pretzel crab melts, sweet and tangy barbecue meatballs, berry honey-lavender funnel cakes topped with Chantilly cream, or strawberry shortcake Liège waffles. Don't forget to wet your whistle, because the beverage game is also strong, with blueberry boba tea, blue woog, and passion fruit lemonade being just some of the offerings. The festival runs from April until June—exact dates vary per year—and with everything available, it's the perfect recipe for a fun-filled day.

▶ *Park Pointers*

Wondering how Dollywood hosts have so many beautiful plants in full bloom and ready to go on the first day of the festival? The work actually starts months in advance, with the flowers grown and tended to in greenhouses before being transported to the park for installation. Each festival gets better than the last, with recent years seeing more than 1 million beautiful blossoms on display. On the hillside bordering the walkway between Craftsman's Valley and The Village, you can see a Smoky Mountain nature scene fashioned from a plush carpet of 37,000 flowers. The festival decor is carefully selected to reflect symbols of the Smokies—like black bears, butterflies, ducks, and bees—along with personal connections to Dolly's life.

 ## Coat of Many Colors Mosaiculture

Dolly's 1971 song "Coat of Many Colors" tells a heartwarming story from her childhood. It's about her mama sewing a coat from a box of mismatched rags to keep young Dolly warm. The floral sculpture by the same name (on display during the festival) illustrates Dolly's mama sewing her coat.

3. Smoky Mountain Summer Celebration

═══ FAST FACTS ═══

WHAT: Embrace the hottest time of the year with this sizzling fiesta of feasts, fun, and fabulous visual showcases.

WHERE: Looping from the park gates to the tippy top of Craftsman's Valley and back again, you'll find manifestations of the sunny season everywhere you go.

EXPERT TIP: With a two-park season pass, you can start the day cooling off at Splash Country, and then finish off a full day of summer fun with the festival at Dollywood.

▶ Why You Should See It

Dollywood's Smoky Mountain Summer Celebration is the ultimate feel-good festival. One favorite is the *Gazillion Bubble Show* at DP's Celebrity Theater. With bubbles larger-than-life and even a full-on bubble blizzard, it's like stepping into a dream. Once you have bubbles on the brain, try out the Bubble Foam Zone in Wilderness Pass to cool off while being blasted by foamy bubbles. You'll feel like you're taking a bubble bath without water! And don't forget to look up: Dollywood's summer sky above Showstreet becomes a canvas for citrus-hued kites soaring overhead. Keep your gaze upward when you get to the top of Craftsman's Valley to see hundreds of suspended pool noodles that transform the trees above into a riot of color. At night, head to Wildwood Grove for Sweet Summer Nights. Go a little early to join in on a family-friendly dance party complete with lighting effects and a live DJ (for exact times, check updated schedules online or via the Dollywood app before you go). At the end of the party, the DJ counts down to one of the most spectacular sights you'll ever see: a combination fireworks and drone show. In the evening sky, 500 lighted drones come together to create a series of unbelievable animated shapes. You'll see butterflies' gently flapping wings, twirling spirals, shooting stars, and more. Capping off the show is a thunderous fireworks display set to music guaranteed to have you feeling emotional and fulfilled by your fun-filled day.

The festival isn't just a feast for the eyes and ears; it's a feast for your taste buds too! When it comes to delightful summertime eats, Dollywood knows how to keep your belly as happy as your heart. Sample savory picks like a four-cheese open-faced grilled cheese sandwich, Southern fried corn on the cob, or pork belly on a stick. Wash everything down with some mountain berry lemonade or a blue coconut Fresca, and then indulge in a sweet finish with a s'mores funnel cake, peanut butter cup Liège waffle, or special festival cannoli. You can find the limited-time festival dishes either at dedicated seasonal booths or on special menus at existing establishments. When you're nice and full, take in one of the street performers like Liquid Beats, a percussion group that uses garden tools and buckets as their instruments. While listening, cool off under the oversized bouquet of colorful garden hoses spraying down Market Square. If you're a fan of classic rock songs, Hydro Jive Junction is a high-energy group that'll have you groovin' to summery favorites from the 1950s.

▶ Park Pointers

Be sure to dress in clothing that can get wet and dries quickly (or bring a change of clothes), because between the water rides, splash play areas, and festival-specific soaking fun, you're not likely to get through the whole day dry! The silver lining is that there is ample opportunity to cool off from the Tennessee heat. If you stay late for Sweet Summer Nights, a sea of people will all be heading for the park gates at the same time. To make your escape go a little faster, consider leaving before the fireworks finish to beat the rush.

4. Harvest Festival

──────── FAST FACTS ────────

WHAT: A pumpkin-spiced, leaf-crunching bash where warm fall vibes meet spooky season aesthetics.

WHERE: The autumnal atmosphere blankets every part of the park during the day, while the Halloween spirit comes alive after the sun goes down.

EXPERT TIP: Fall temperatures in Tennessee run the gamut from balmy to freezing. Dress in layers that you can peel off or add to as the weather changes.

▶ Why You Should See It

That first fall crispness in the air feels like nature's way of rewarding you for surviving another sweltering summer, so grab your coziest sweater and celebrate at Dollywood's Harvest Festival. Right through the gate you'll walk under Showstreet's Harvest Sky, an expansive curtain of fluttering leaves in hues of honeyed yellow and saffron. See the mammoth-sized pumpkin tree in Market Square or touch *massive* pumpkins on display from farmers throughout the region (some weighing over 1,000 pounds!). Craftsman's Valley becomes even more incredible during this festival, as elite artisans from across the country visit to share their crafts, including expert pumpkin carving! Meet brand-new characters to hug and take photos with, like a friendly scarecrow named Patches, or the jolly Pumpkin Master with his gourd-covered orange top hat. And because this is Dollywood, there are plenty of special live shows to celebrate the festival's welcoming tone. When the sun goes to sleep and the moon takes over, Great Pumpkin LumiNights illuminates the park with the spine-tingling glow of over 12,000 pumpkins. Each area of the park sports a different theme. See carved pumpkin "quilts" and a massive jack-o'-lantern guitar at Craftsman's Valley, walk beneath hooting owls and an archway of midnight-purple bats in Timber Canyon, check out adorable "pumpkin people" scenes in The Village, and so much more.

Now for the part you've been waiting for: the food! Get ready to embark on a mouthwatering journey that's all about celebrating the most flavor-packed season of the year. Warm up with a bowl of pumpkin bisque with toasted pepitas or three-bean pumpkin chili, or sink your teeth into a salted maple potato tornado or a pumpkin sausage and ricotta pizza. Autumn apple palmer, pumpkin pie punch, and hot wassail lead the liquid refreshment list. Dessert selections may include a decadent pumpkin pie funnel cake, a thick and creamy pumpkin spice milkshake, or a Belgian waffle Heath bar ice cream sandwich. Fall is when some of the most amazing baked items are created in kitchens across the South, so don't pass up browsing the display cases in Spotlight Bakery for pumpkin whoopie pies, adorable cookies decorated with falling leaves and jack-o'-lanterns, caramel apple Danishes, and jumbo cupcakes and muffins. The menus change and are expanded every single year, so this list is just a small sample of what you might find.

▶ Park Pointers

If you're trying to plan your Smoky Mountain trip to see the peak of the fall foliage, it can be hard to predict and largely depends on when the temperatures start to consistently nosedive. Mid-October is a fairly safe choice to see some pretty leaves and enjoy the bulk of the Harvest Festival. If you have young kids, waiting for darkness to set in to enjoy the lights can make for a long day. For season passholders or those with multiday tickets, choosing one day to not arrive until sunset helps keep everyone's energy levels up when the pumpkins finally come to life. You'll probably have time to hit a few rides as a bonus too.

5. Smoky Mountain Christmas

WHAT: This festival transforms Dollywood into a twinkling fantasyland of yuletide beauty.

WHERE: You won't have to travel to the North Pole for this jolly affair; you just have to get to Dollywood! The entire park gets in on the fun.

EXPERT TIP: Arrive early for the Christmas tree show and claim one of the rocking chairs near outdoor heaters. Best and comfiest seat in the house!

▶ Why You Should See It

Dollywood's Smoky Mountain Christmas festival is the bee's knees of holiday celebrations! With millions of dazzling lights, the scent of freshly baked gingerbread cookies in the air, and a chorus of carolers spreading cheer, it's where the spirit of Christmas runs free. After dark is when the enchanting decor schemes themed to each area become obvious. The Village and Showstreet show off with traditional red, green, and gold trimming, along with lush garlands and bells. Owens Farm, Rivertown Junction, and Craftsman's Valley mimic a candlelight glow with warm white lights, and the area leading from Craftsman's Valley to The Village features a 130-foot light wall. Country Fair is where you'll find Peppermint Valley, a forest of red and white trees. Enjoy a retro Christmas in Jukebox Junction with multicolor jumbo bulbs and old-fashioned tinsel. Wilderness Pass and Timber Canyon are where things get arctic with the Glacier Ridge holiday area and its white and blue lights, animated icicles, illuminated polar bears, and a 130-foot light tunnel. Some evenings, you can end your celebration with the "Merry & Bright!" fireworks display. The must-see holiday attraction, though, is the tremendously popular storytelling music and light show on a 50-foot animated Christmas tree. The show repeats every half hour and ends with a snowy surprise! Wildwood Grove steps outside tradition with colored lights incorporating unconventional shimmery pinks and purples in the fanciful displays.

While you're enjoying all this merriment, take your palate on a mouthwatering sleigh ride: Dollywood's Christmas menu is a ho-ho-holiday treat whose every scrumptious bite you'll want to sample! Spoil yourself with gingerbread churros dipped in peppermint eggnog sauce, Belgian waffle ice cream sandwiches dipped in chocolate and coated with crushed peppermint, eggnog cheesecake with a gingersnap crust, and your choice of ice cream flavor in a gingerbread cone. Dollywood elves are hard at work in Spotlight Bakery making hot chocolate and sugar cookie cupcakes and a whole host of beautifully iced cookies to enjoy in the park or take home for holiday parties. For the main event, you might find Christmas toastie sandwiches (basically a whole turkey and stuffing dinner inside a roll), chipotle turkey nachos, Southern-style chicken potpie in a golden crispy bread cone, loaded creamy potato soup, and candied pork belly skillets. Jovial thirst quenchers include chilled peppermint hot cocoa, holiday limeade, and a concoction of tangy cranberry and orange.

▶ Park Pointers

The live shows are bursting full of holiday cheer with a whole new lineup of performers, costumes, set decor, and lights. Check schedules and come up with a game plan at the beginning of the day to have a better chance of seeing everything you want. It's helpful to finish up with rides, shows, and other festival activities during daylight so you can spend the entire evening enjoying the holiday lights. There's one ride you *should* wait until night to experience, though: the train. The Dollywood Express during the festival is a completely new experience. Bop along to Christmas music, join in on a sing-along, and brace yourself for a literal field of oscillating colored lights.

CHAPTER TEN

Other Dolly Properties

Dolly Parton isn't just the Queen of Country Music and Dollywood's Dreamer in Chief, she's also the monarch of other marvelous destinations! At Dollywood's Splash Country, you can cool down and get wet in a full-blown water park that'll have you feeling like a kid again. And for those who prefer their supper with a show, there's Dolly Parton's Stampede Dinner Attraction just down the road a bit from the theme and water parks. Hoping to stay close by during your visit? She's got the Dollywood's DreamMore Resort and Spa and the brand-new Dollywood's HeartSong Lodge & Resort, where you can kick back and soak in the Smoky Mountain charm. You can even have a bougie stay in her swanky retired tour bus! Dolly sure knows how to make an entire world of magic.

1. Dolly Parton's Stampede Dinner Attraction

═══ FAST FACTS ═══

WHAT: A spellbinding four-course dinner and show featuring dazzling horsemanship, stunts, and musical performances.

WHERE: This attraction is located one block south of Dollywood Lane on the Pigeon Forge Parkway. Look for the red barn building!

EXPERT TIP: Book tickets early for peak season (holidays, summer) shows and don't forget to bring cash if you want to leave a tip for your server!

▶ Why You Should See It

Dolly Parton's Stampede Dinner Attraction is a rootin'-tootin' good time! The open end of the horseshoe-shaped theater features a rocky structure in front of a large screen that resembles a western landscape. The seating is tiered, so there's no such thing as a bad view. When buying tickets, you'll get to choose whether you want to sit on the North side or the South side; this is the team you'll be cheering for during the friendly competition parts of the event. Instructed to stomp your feet when your mouth and hands are too full of food to cheer and clap, the show begins, and it's a nonstop blend of jaw-dropping stunts (some of which include fire), equestrian prowess, dazzling costumes, and rib-tickling comedy all topped off with a generous helping of Southern charm.

The homestyle dinner is served while the show proceeds. Drink orders are taken first, and you'll be sipping straight from a Mason jar. Servers move down the line of tables multiple times, adding one item to your plate at a time. First up is Stampede's famous creamy vegetable soup served with a hot, fluffy biscuit. And no, there's not a spoon to be found: The soup is meant to be sipped directly from a bowl (don't worry, there's a handle), and that biscuit should be dunked right in for maximum effect. The main course has you tearing into a roasted Cornish hen with crispy, golden skin; a hickory-smoked pork loin; corn on the cob; and half of a buttery herbed potato. Again, everything is designed to be finger-food friendly, so don't be shy, and dig right in. Dessert is usually a hot apple turnover or similar sweet treat (again, something easy to eat with your hands).

▶ Park Pointers

Arrive early for the show and take advantage of the Horse Walk! Performance horses in the show are led to the outdoor stables and you can walk along the stalls, take photos, and see their beauty up close. Signs above each horse display their name, breed, and some info about them. The horses are groomed twice a day—before and after performing—and the riders themselves are involved with grooming and exercising the powerful animals to further strengthen the bond they share. Dolly is serious about the well-being of horses used in tourism, so the thirty-two horse performers are rotated in and out throughout the season and turned out to pasture for some much-needed R & R. They have access to around-the-clock veterinary care provided by the University of Tennessee to keep them in prime health whether they're executing a routine or frolicking through the grass.

 ### Name Change

Prior to 2018, Dolly Parton's Stampede Dinner Attraction was known as Dixie Stampede. Dolly told *Billboard* that when she was made aware of the problematic nature of the name, she promptly changed it.

Splash Country
2. Big Bear Plunge

WHAT: Family "white water" downhill raft ride. Riders must be 36 inches tall, and those under 48 inches must be accompanied by someone age 14 or older.

WHERE: Cross the far bridge over the lazy river and hang an immediate left. Follow the path around, bearing left until you see the sign in front of you along with the stairway to the top.

EXPERT TIP: It's worth it to rent a locker when you get to the park so all your loose items will be safely stowed away and you can ride all day without worry!

▶ Why You Should See It

Big Bear Plunge at Dollywood's Splash Country is the ultimate family water adventure! It's like taking a wild ride down fast-moving Smoky Mountain streams, with twists, turns, and tunnels. It's the kind of ride that leaves you grinning, screaming, and wanting to turn around and do it again. While the water channel doesn't exactly look like a rock-studded mountain river, you'll certainly feel as if that's exactly where you are. After climbing to the top of the 70-foot attraction, you and two or three of your closest friends or family members will pile into the river tube. It'll be all knees and elbows in there, so sitting "crisscross applesauce" is the best approach for the most comfort. Hold on tight to the handles on top! When you shove off, you'll zip down the track like a rocket and straight into a tunnel. When you emerge, you'll quickly understand how this ride got its name as you plunge down the first hill and then are immediately sent into another tunnel. After navigating hairpin turns and lightning-fast straightaways, if you're not wet enough yet, that problem is remedied when you crash through a water curtain and down a bumpy drop before splashing into the splash pool at the bottom.

▶ Park Pointers

Big Bear Plunge opened for adventurers during the 2004 season. Each river tube requires a minimum of three riders and a maximum of four. If you are riding alone or with one other person, you will be paired with another group, so if you're iffy about riding with strangers, that's something to keep in mind. Conversely, if you have a larger group, you'll be separated into different tubes. If you love this ride, you'll also enjoy Raging River Rapids, another family-style rafting ride in Splash Country. It's similar to Big Bear Plunge, but each raft can hold up to five riders, the channel is longer, there are no tunnels, and the drops aren't quite as steep. You can find Raging River Rapids by following the path you used to Big Bear Plunge all the way to the opposite side of the park, just past The Butterfly body slides. For safety reasons, Big Bear Plunge will close when lightning is detected within a 10-mile radius of the park.

Safety First

Splash Country provides life vests at no charge for nonswimmers and small children. No outside water wings, pool toys, or flotation devices are allowed. Slip-on shoes are encouraged for hot concrete, and don't forget sunscreen!

Splash Country
3. Fire Tower Falls

═══ FAST FACTS ═══

WHAT: The park's fastest twin waterslides! Riders must be at least 48 inches tall.

WHERE: Located toward the far end of the park between the Mountain Waves pool and the leisurely Cascades pool.

EXPERT TIP: To get the most speed out of the slide, wear formfitting swimwear (as opposed to baggy swim trunks or swim skirts) to reduce drag on the way down.

▶ Why You Should See It

Reminiscent of a real fire tower with a staircase that winds around and up to the top, this attraction gives you a commanding panoramic view of the surrounding land. You may even forget that you're about to throw yourself down the steep 70-foot slide when you get to the top and are hit with views of the lush greenery of the Smokies and of Dollywood's DreamMore Resort and Spa on an adjacent hill. The rushing water is already tumbling over the slide, so all that's left to do is scramble on, lie back, cross your arms over your chest, and *gooo*! There's no buildup of speed because as soon as you slide away from the edge, you're shooting straight down. Be sure to keep your mouth closed while speeding along in a near free fall, and it's also a good idea to hold your breath to avoid inhaling water as you hit the bottom. Fire Tower Falls is a body slide, meaning your body actually makes contact with the surface, and no tube, board, or other flotation device is used. Cotton shirts, cover-ups, or shoes of any kind are not allowed on this ride for safety reasons (rash guards are okay).

▶ *Park Pointers*

This attraction debuted in 2006, and its construction opened up a second pathway from the far end of the park to the center section and Mountain Waves pool. Fire Tower Falls will close when lightning is detected within a 10-mile radius of the park. Once you get your breath back after climbing off the slide, you'll be right next door to the serene waters of The Cascades, a low-key pool and activity area with slides that wind through a rock grotto, plus a 20-foot-tall geyser, water jets and bubblers, and plenty of deck space for enjoying the sun. On the opposite side of the Falls attraction is the ultimate splash pad: Bear Mountain Fire Tower. This splash 'n' slide family area has seven slides, sprayers and cannons, and a gargantuan dump bucket that slowly fills up before tipping over and soaking everyone in sight! If you're a big fan of body slides or if Fire Tower Falls looks a little too intense, try The Butterfly, a similar steep body slide with a much-shorter (55-foot) drop into a butterfly-shaped pool. There's also Mountain Scream, a triple body slide where you can choose from a twisty tunnel or an open-air plummet with four bumpy "mini drops" on the way to the ground.

Lost Something?

It's easier than you think to leave or drop something when having fun, especially on water rides when any loose items are a big no-no! Dollywood and Splash Country share a Lost and Found window where you can drop off or find forgotten items. The window is located near Guest Services and Doggywood at the front gates of Dollywood, or you can file a claim online.

Splash Country
4. SwiftWater Run

FAST FACTS

WHAT: A moderately intense bowl-style waterslide you can ride alone or with a buddy. Riders must be at least 48 inches tall. Single tubes have a weight limit of 250 pounds, and double tubes have a combined weight limit of 400 pounds.

WHERE: The big green and yellow spiral is easy to see tucked between the splash pools of Raging River Rapids and Mountain Scream.

EXPERT TIP: This is the closest thing to a "spinning" ride at Splash Country, so if you are sensitive to dizziness, take a pass on this one.

▶ Why You Should See It

SwiftWater Run gives you a front-row seat to what it's like to be sucked into the churning waters of a whirlpool while having the time of your life! With the height requirement, older children (around 8 years old or so) should be able to ride but may not be ready for this one quite yet. After walking to the top of the structure, you settle into your tube. You can embark on the adventure alone or take a friend along in a double-seater. Once ready, you'll be sent on your way down a high-speed tunnel that brings you to the bottom of a hill, around a curve, and into a large bowl that's open to the sky. Your only job is to hold on to the handles on the side of the tube to keep yourself steady, but other than that, just go with the flow and enjoy the journey! You'll zip around the perimeter once...twice...then a third time before getting sucked into the exit hole at the center. You'll then go down a short little bunny hill and through a water curtain and splash down in the shallow pool at the bottom. This is a quick ride that takes less than one minute, so if you come to the park on a less busy day, you can get right back in line and thrill to it over and over again!

▶ Park Pointers

SwiftWater Run was announced in October 2007 and set to open the following season, in May 2008. Dolly recognized the lack of "spinny" rides in the water park and figured that this new attraction would fix the problem right up. SwiftWater Run will close when lightning is detected within a 10-mile radius of the park. If you're ready to try another one of Splash Country's more intense slides, go over to RiverRush, Tennessee's very first—and for now, the only—water coaster! It features four stories of drops, tunnels, and crazy turns. If you've had enough of the fast stuff and are ready to relax, it might be time to grab a lounger at Mountain Waves, a 25,000-square-foot wave pool whose waves ripple mildly through the sparkling water.

TimeSaver H2O

Visiting Splash Country on a crowded day? Consider purchasing a TimeSaver H2O pass to gain access to a faster queue. You can choose between two levels: a combination of eight attractions or an unlimited number of rides, giving you speedy access to your favorite thrills all day long.

Splash Country
5. Slick Rock Racer

WHAT: Race your friends down a quadruple-lane waterslide and try to be the first to hit the bottom! Riders must be at least 42 inches tall.

WHERE: Head to the far corner of the park, behind Mountain Twist, and take a long stroll up the hillside to reach the top of the slide.

EXPERT TIP: Wanna win? Make yourself as aerodynamic as possible by keeping your head down and your feet together when you shove off from the platform.

▶ Why You Should See It

As you work your way up the long nature-enveloped trail to the official ride queue, you might find yourself engaging in some friendly trash talk with your pals while watching the current riders speed down the slides next to you. Oh, and you'll be hauling your own mat up the hill with you, but don't worry, it doesn't weigh much. At the end of the path there's a short staircase to climb, and then you're finally there. When it's your turn, pick a lane, place your mat down, and climb on...face down! There are two little handles under the curved end of the mat that you'll grasp during the slide. (You'll feel like you're lying on the ground propped up on your elbows.) After scooching yourself away from the edge, it'll only take about twenty-five seconds to traverse the 300-foot slide before coming to a semi-gentle stop in the shallow splash pool at the bottom. It's not all straight down and splashety-splash, though: You'll bump your way over three separate drops (including the push-off from the top) to help build up speed. You won't go underwater when you reach the end, but you'll probably get a good dousing right in the face, so be prepared!

▶ Park Pointers

Slick Rock Racer has been sending Splash Country guests screaming down the hillside since May 2010. The ride will close when lightning strikes are detected within a 10-mile radius of the park. Did you find yourself coming in last place and need a rematch? Exact revenge on the buddy (or buddies!) who bested you and challenge them to a ride on TailSpin Racer located near the park gates. TailSpin is a six-lane mat race waterslide with the same height requirement as Slick Rock's, but with a little extra excitement tossed into the mix, as the race starts inside a tunnel. You won't know who is in the lead until you all emerge on the other side to make that last push for the finish line.

What's in a Name?

Having grown up in the mountains, Dolly knows a thing or two about slippery rocks! When she and her siblings played in the creeks surrounding her Locust Ridge home, she remembers landing on a mossy rock and being sent for a ride...straight into the water! Those memories were the inspiration for Slick Rock Racer.

Splash Country
6. Wild River Falls

WHAT: Single or double tube raft ride with four slides that all provide a slightly different adventure. Riders must be at least 36 inches tall to ride, and those under 48 inches must be accompanied by someone age 14 or older. Single rider weight limit of 300 pounds. Double rider weight limit of 500 pounds; one rider must be between 36 and 50 inches tall.

WHERE: Entrance to the ride queue is up the path a smidge from The Butterfly and across from the splash pool of Raging River Rapids.

EXPERT TIP: Try each color of slide so you can determine which is your favorite!

▶ Why You Should See It

The soaking treatment starts early, because you'll go through a water curtain right at the mouth of the slide regardless of which color you pick. Each color starts in a closed tube, and the orange and green slides stay that way for the duration, giving you one last soaking with another water wall at the very end. The outer slides—blue and yellow—change things up a bit. The yellow slide starts out inside a tunnel, sending you twisting and turning. Then you endure a second soaking from another water curtain before bursting into the sunlight in an open channel, going through several more turns with your tube tilting up the side of the half-pipe. Hopping aboard the blue slide sends you on a peekaboo ride of both tunnels and open air (you'll go through two water curtains with this slide too). Skimming into the pool at the end is gentler than expected, but you'll feel a good splash when you hit. Your tube will naturally drift over to the side for an easy exit. The water is 3 feet deep, so most riders will be able to hop out and walk over to the edge, but keep an eye on smaller children that are near the minimum height requirement (a lifeguard is also nearby).

▶ Park Pointers

Wild River Falls opened right along with the water park in 2001. The ability to ride in a double tube with a child is a great opportunity to give a little courage to a young rider who is new to bigger water rides. Wild River Falls will close when lightning is detected within 10 miles of the park. When you exit the slides, there's a great lookout point straight ahead where you can gaze down on Downbound Float Trip—Splash Country's huge lazy river! Guests float in an inflatable tube or walk along and enjoy this endless loop of relaxing, slow-moving water. Put on your sunglasses, lie back on your tube, and enjoy the sunshine and lulling motion of the water. But don't worry if there's a little rain in the forecast! As long as there's no lightning, a drizzly day can be the perfect time to visit Splash Country, and you may even score some shorter lines. Hey, you came to get wet anyway, right?

A Fan Named the Park!

Dolly held a public contest to name her brand-new water park, resulting in over 16,000 submitted ideas. The winning name— Dolly's Splash Country—was suggested by a man named John Torres. He and his family won five years of season passes and an autographed canoe. In 2004, the name was altered to Dolly- wood's Splash Country.

Splash Country
7. Campsite Grill

WHAT: The best and biggest place in Splash Country for hot pool-area food and snacks.

WHERE: You'll find the Grill across from the "beach" entrance to the lazy river and behind Little Creek Falls, a zero-depth family splash pad.

EXPERT TIP: For those with two-park season passes, add the water park dining pass option for one free meal and snack per day per pass. Look for blue and red diamonds on menu boards to see which items qualify.

▶ Why You Should See It

This rustic building with its red tin roof and wood and stone facade is mighty inviting when you start feeling peckish during a long day in the sun. The menu here is teeming with favorite poolside classics. Hot options are cheeseburgers, grilled chicken sandwiches, and Buffalo or regular chicken tenders, all served with fries. Pepperoni or plain cheese pizzas can be ordered personal- or (16-inch) family-sized. If you're just feeling a little snacky, choose from single-order French fries, fruit cups, chips, or pretzel sticks with Cheddar cheese dipping sauce. For something sweet, there are cookies, banana pudding, or cookies and cream pudding. Special dietary needs are taken into consideration at Campsite Grill, and a few menu alterations can be made: You can request your burger be served on a gluten-free bun with a meatless burger patty, or try a gluten-free and plant-based pizza. With grub in hand, choose from the smattering of picnic tables available behind the rows and rows of loungers lining the lazy river, so it won't take you long to get right back to water play once you're done eating. Just remember to wait at least half an hour before getting back in the water, like Mama always says.

▶ Park Pointers

While the main Dollywood park is where you'll find serious Southern eatin', Splash Country's collection of quick service stands will keep you from going hungry. On the back side of Campsite Grill's building, you'll find cold to-go lunch meals at Picnic in the Park. Deli sandwiches and wraps, salads, and other snacks are quick, on-the-go possibilities here, as well as a selection of frozen ICEEs when the heat gets to be a little too much. Five of Splash Country's food stops are located on the "island" inside of the huge lazy river—Dippin' Dots, Campsite Grill, Picnic in the Park, Blended Pedaler, and Fill & Chill. The rest are peppered around the main pools and play areas, including the water park's version of Dogs N Taters and, down by itself near the park gates, Big River Pavilion, with its popular pulled pork sandwiches. Other nibbles perfect for lounging, like nachos, burritos, tacos, butterfly pretzels, chocolate-covered frozen bananas, and popcorn, can be bought at the various concession stands scattered around the park. While you can't find cinnamon bread in Splash Country, you do have a chance to try its own exclusive cinnamon sugar treat all the way from Canada: BeaverTails! Ovals of dough are stretched by hand to resemble the tail of a beaver, deep-fried until crisp, and topped with your choice of candy, fruit, or sweet spreads. Splash Country does not allow outside food other than one unopened water bottle per person or baby supplies, but you'll never be farther than a couple minutes' walk from a place to grab some great grub.

8. Dollywood's DreamMore Resort and Spa

━━━━━━━ **FAST FACTS** ━━━━━━━

WHAT: In appreciation of family time, storytelling, and Southern heritage, this is Dollywood's first full-sized resort.

WHERE: The glowing white buildings of the complex are located just across the street from Splash Country, between Dollywood Resorts Boulevard and Veterans Boulevard.

EXPERT TIP: Don't miss the massive breakfast buffet at Song & Hearth from 7 a.m. to 11 a.m., Monday through Saturday, and 7:30 a.m. to 12 p.m. on Sundays.

▶ Why You Should See It

Dollywood's DreamMore Resort and Spa is a place where hospitality meets elegance, so every moment is a special memory in the making! Choose from standard rooms, junior suites, and family suites for those who need room to spread out. Oh, and if you really want to dip your toes into luxury, you can stay in the Dolly Parton Suite, a penthouse apartment where Dolly herself stays when she visits the resort! Every square inch of this crown jewel suite is decorated to the hilt and includes a bed fit for a queen, an absolutely palatial master bathroom, a private office, a walk-in closet, and more. DreamMore's full-service spa has everything you need to spoil yourself with pampering, like haircuts and styling, facial treatments, massages, waxing, manicures, and pedicures.

Epicureans will not find themselves disappointed at Song & Hearth: A Southern Eatery, the resort's warm and cozy restaurant. Breakfast and dinner buffets are served in the rustic-chic dining room, and there is so much to taste and try, with courses spanning several rooms. Between meals, relax next to one of the resort's glittering pools—one indoor and one outdoor—or watch the kids play in the splash pad. Later that night, switch to the hot tub after picking up some snacks at DM Pantry. Dollywood is a dry park, but DreamMore is where you can go for creative signature cocktails at The Lounge, the swanky-meets-country bar on-site.

▶ Park Pointers

Enjoy exclusive perks for being a guest at the resort! Every visitor with a Dollywood ticket receives a free TimeSaver pass for expedited entry into select rides as well as unlimited priority seating at live shows. If you have Dollywood or Splash Country tickets and your stay includes a Saturday, you'll be able to enter the park an hour earlier than the public. And there is a free shuttle to and from the park, picking you up from the resort and dropping you off right at the park gates, then bringing you back to the resort at the end of the day. Save on the cost and hassle of parking yourself! Speaking of parking, self-park at the resort is free for all guests. And don't worry about hauling around all the souvenirs you buy, because you can have everything sent directly to the resort so that it's waiting for you whenever you get back ($25 purchase minimum required).

Her Place in History

In 2015, the year the resort opened, Dolly wrote a special song called "My Place in History." She recorded the song onto a CD and included it, along with a CD player, in a locked chestnut box that's kept in a glass case behind a velvet rope at the resort. The song will be released on her one hundredth birthday in 2046.

9. Dolly Suite 1986

FAST FACTS

WHAT: The ultimate experience for Dolly fans! Enjoy a stay in her decked-out retired tour bus and a gourmet dinner customized just for you.

WHERE: The bus is parked behind a locked wrought iron gate on the premises of Dollywood's DreamMore Resort and Spa.

EXPERT TIP: Dolly had a custom-designed shower installed in the bus just for her, including a miniature bathtub. Dolly is a tiny little thing herself and can fit in there better than most, but you owe it to yourself to squeeze inside and bathe like country music royalty!

▶ Why You Should See It

Live like Dolly by staying in the *actual* tour bus that she used from 2008 until its retirement in March 2022. Now simply called Suite 1986, in reference to the year Dollywood opened to the public, the bus is stationary after traveling over 360,000 miles during its tenure. A stay in Dolly's luxury Prevost motor coach doesn't come cheap, with packages starting at $10,000 for a two-night stay. The package doesn't only include the stay in the bus—which can accommodate a maximum of two guests—but also comes with a whole slew of fun perks. The price includes a room in the main resort that sleeps up to four additional people and tickets to both Dollywood and Dollywood's Splash Country. As a guest of the Suite, enjoy the swag waiting for you on the buttery-leather dinette decorated with sequined throw pillows.

The take-home loot includes a variety of Dolly's vinyl albums, luxury bath products, matching bathrobes, and Dolly's signature perfume. The kitchen area includes a microwave-convection oven, a sink, and a small pantry next to the surprisingly large refrigerator (stocked with soft drinks). The surfaces are wine colored and flecked with gold, there are tassels hanging from the windows, and the whole place just screams, "Dolly was here!" In the very back of the bus, along with the bright pink bed, there are a refrigerator and freezer with ornately carved doors, a mini microwave, and a TV with a surround sound system. You have access to Dolly's personal bathroom (separate from the guest bathroom, even on a bus!) as well as a chance to peer behind glass at some of her personal effects, like a guitar and select items from her wardrobe. There's even a wig cabinet!

Along with a delicious cheese board waiting for you when you arrive, you and your guest will be treated to an elegant multicourse dinner at the resort that can be customized to fit your individual tastes or dietary needs. Whiskey-glazed bacon-wrapped shrimp with andouille sausage over stone-ground grits might be the first plate that's placed in front of you, followed by, perhaps, a burrata caprese salad. The main course might be something along the lines of mesquite-smoked brisket, hickory pulled pork, or Song & Hearth's expertly fried chicken. Side dishes include a generous portion of collard greens, mac and cheese, sweet potato purée, Yukon smashed potatoes, and those hot, fluffy biscuits that absolutely cannot be forgotten. Each course includes an expert wine pairing and an exquisite dessert finish of bourbon crème brûlée, pecan pralines, or one of Dolly's all-time favorites: banana pudding. After such a decadent culinary adventure, you'll be ready to curl up between Dolly's sheets and have sweet dreams.

▶ Park Pointers

Dolly didn't start traveling in her bus straight off the assembly line. Some "minor" adjustments had to be made first! A full-sized refrigerator was moved in—the windshield had to be removed to install it—as well as a bathtub-shower combo with custom glass door emblazoned with "Dolly."

Three of the original six bunks were removed to create an extra closet for Dolly's wardrobe. The entire interior was custom painted with murals of caravan travelers to reflect Dolly's love of living on the road, and every inch of the decor, right down to the elegant floor tiles and rich colors that bathe the whole space, shows how Dolly's specific vision for her rolling home was brought to life.

 ## The Dollywood Foundation

Profits from the Suite are donated to the Dollywood Foundation, a nonprofit organization founded in 1988. Its flagship program is Dolly Parton's Imagination Library that mails a free book to every enrolled child (*all* children can enroll in eligible areas) every single month from birth to age 5. As of March 2024, over 230 million books have been donated!

10. Dollywood's HeartSong Lodge & Resort

═══ FAST FACTS ═══

WHAT: A newer resort celebrating everything that makes the Smokies special and encouraging guests to seek out their own heart song.

WHERE: Just down the road a piece from Dollywood's Dream-More Resort and Spa on Dollywood Resorts Boulevard.

EXPERT TIP: Floor plans for every single room type are available online—check them out so you are sure to get the perfect lodging setup for you and your group!

▶ Why You Should See It

This resort opened in the fall of 2023. When you step into the 4,000-square-foot atrium lobby, stop and look up. The four-story stone fireplace stretches toward the cathedral ceiling, and there's an ornate custom fireplace grate showing a wrought iron likeness of Dolly as a child sitting on a tree branch among autumn leaves and butterflies. Choices for accommodation include standard rooms with or without a balcony that can sleep up to four guests or specialized suites that can accommodate families or larger groups. Behind the resort you'll find a pool with a chattering waterfall (there's a pool indoors as well), a large hot tub, several firepits with comfortable seating for conversation on cool nights, lawn games, and play areas.

When it's time to eat, there are plenty of options. Ember & Elm, the resort's anchor restaurant, is refined and elegant while still comfortable and welcoming, with warm earth tones cooled down by deep blues. The table service menu includes breakfast and dinner—a continental breakfast is also available—and signature dishes are crafted using locally sourced ingredients. Your meal could include a Tennessee creamery cheese and charcuterie board with a bowl of butternut and poblano soup, followed by beef short ribs in a red wine reduction or shrimp and scallop grits. Other culinary options include High Note, a comfy retreat for casual dining and drinks; Cove Poolside Dining; and Songbird Market for quick-grab snacks and sweets (including Dollywood cinnamon bread!), as well as Starbucks beverages.

▶ Park Pointers

Dolly's influence suffuses this splendid addition to Dollywood's collection of resorts. The grand porte cochere in front of the resort, surrounded by rock and water features reminiscent of a Smoky Mountain creek, is only the beginning of what you'll find inside. You'll discover hints of Dolly (color, a little glam, a few butterflies) and hints of what makes the Smoky Mountains so incredible (fireflies, trees, babbling creeks, wildlife, and serenity). Guests at HeartSong enjoy all the same park perks as those at DreamMore. Ticket holders receive a free TimeSaver pass for expedited entry into select rides as well as unlimited priority seating at live shows. If your stay includes a Saturday, you'll be able to enter Dollywood or Splash Country an hour earlier than non-resort guests. The free shuttle to and from the park lets you bypass having to deal with the time and cost of parking on-site (plus, self-parking at HeartSong is free for all guests). If you spend at least $25 in the parks, you can have your items sent directly to the resort and you won't have to carry them around all day.

Distinct Theming

DreamMore was inspired by places Dolly could call home, while HeartSong was inspired by a place that Dolly could go to relax, to let her soul sing.

Index

Note: Page numbers in **bold** indicate maps.

About the Author

Erin K. Browne is the blogger and photographer behind *Brownie Bites*, where she shares approachable, easy recipes that are as fun to make as they are to eat. She especially loves pop culture and fandom-inspired recipes, with Dollywood being a major source of such inspiration—the park is just a short drive from her home. Outside of the kitchen, Erin enjoys reading in a cozy chair, hiking in the mountains, and exploring the country in her family's RV. She currently lives in Knoxville, Tennessee, with her husband, Matt; her two children, Jasper and Shelby; and her impossibly adorable kitty, Biscuit Fingers. Learn more at BrownieBites.net.

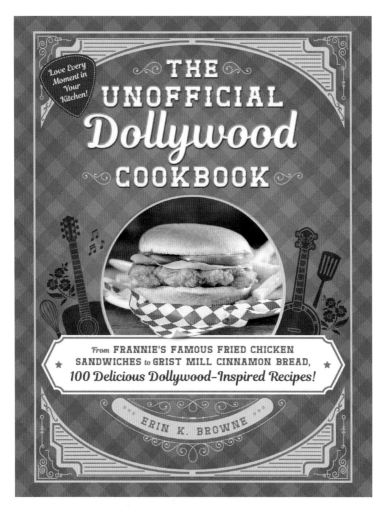